"In a voice almost too
toward the unspeakable
tomless pit of hatred in
essays will spin your head; you will be turned on a dime to his way of thinking."

—Joan d'Arc, Co-Publisher, *Paranoia: The Conspiracy Reader*

"The truth is out there, and John Kaminski knows what it is. The United States of America is facing its greatest challenge since the Civil War. The forces of the criminal elite, the corporadoes and super money are seeking to establish forever their domination of the political, economic and strategic spheres of American life. And they are winning. If we can face it God can fix it. And while many are aware of aspects of the internal corruption of the American State's processes, few are able to comprehend the true extent of the internal problems, let alone map a way out of the mire. In this war against organised criminal politics John Kaminski is one of the shock troops in the most important battle of all, a battle that is taking place on the Internet—THE WAR FOR THE TRUTH. In the original and best sense of the word John Kaminski is a true American patriot."

—Alastair Thompson, Editor, *Scoop* (New Zealand)

"John Kaminski is one of the most important independent voices of sanity in an insane world where corporate media is little more than a propaganda tool being used to keep an unsuspecting public, well, unsuspecting. His writings go a long way in lifting the media veil and exposing not only those who would spoonfeed us their perception of what reality should be, but also exposing what exactly it is they are shielding us from."

—Amanda Garrison, FreeSpeechRadio.net

"John Kaminski is a writer who lays bare the truth, no matter whom it infuriates."

—Bev Conover, editor and publisher of Online Journal,
http://www.onlinejournal.com

"John Kaminski writes what needs to be said and while some will not like what he says, it's only because they don't like the ugly truth and if they read it they may have a conscience to live with."

—Editor LewisNews, www.LewisNews.com & LewisNews Radio

"John Kaminski's trenchant and fearless critiques of the current pathological American political scene have been refreshing and welcome and necessary—for those of us would otherwise have been susceptible to the steady stream of brainwashing coming from the current batch of disinformation-spewing powermongers in Washington, DC. Kaminski sees it and then courageously tells it—like it is, with deep insights, a deep appreciation of history, humor and wisdom. These are classic essays, many of which I have eagerly passed on to others in the faith-based peace and justice movement. Kaminski's insights are not just for these times and this so-called Christian nation, but for those future generations who might smell a rat somewhere and need some help to figure out where the stench is coming from."

—Gary G. Kohls, M.D. for Every Church A Peace Church, http://www.ecapc.org

"John Kaminski cuts through the cancerous tumor that has curled its oily tentacles around the White House like a skilled surgeon, his searing rhetoric accurately backed with facts. Like Noam Chomsky, he should be considered a national treasure among those who still hold out hope of resurrecting the heart and soul of America from the greasy clutches of the cryptocracy."

—B.Z. Botani, Director of MetaMagic Media Volcano, HAWAI'I, http://metamagic.org

"Kaminski presents a shocking yet effectively objective outlook of our current situation. His work points out the cancers destroying the world we live in, and takes shots that expose the foundations of a system in morbid disarray. Revealing a sense of urgency while maintaining the movement's unity, he draws attention to problems far and wide that affect all of us and charts a revolution that we most vow to continue."

—David Marvasti, www.timewedo.com

"'. . . Still, in thousands of emails, that big question keeps coming: What will we do to keep from becoming residents of Camp Ashcroft? Well, here's your answer. Overthrow the government—NOW. We must overthrow the government. There is no other choice. Nothing else will work. Could it be more obvious? We can't use violence, because real humans would be crushed by all the hellish weapons arrayed against the entire world by the military industrial complex that has stolen all our money and erased all our rights under the Constitution. Besides, it is illegal under what's left of the Constitution to advocate the VIOLENT overthrow of the government. And I would never dream of advocating any such thing. It is, however, patently legal and indeed our patriotic duty to advocate the peaceful overthrow of the government. We have to overthrow the government, just like Jefferson said, in a fit of moral outrage, using every bit of our wits and our influence to put these people who are in the process of destroying everything we hold dear in jail. For a long time, if not forever.' (Excerpt from John Kaminski, posted on http://Revolt.net/TheTimeIsNow.htm and included in *America's Autopsy Report*)

"[Statements like these] is why I read John Kaminski. That is why I publish John Kaminski articles throughout the Lovearth Network."

—Mark R. Elsis, Executive Director of the Lovearth Network Connecting through 1000+ EcoHumanePolitical Websites, http://Lovearth.net

"My name is Gina Rinaldi, I'm 16, and I come from England. I just want to say that I have learnt more from reading your articles than I have ever learnt in all my years at school. The best thing about these articles is that it's truth and that is something you can't get from any teacher in schools nowadays. History used to be one of my favorite subjects at school but the more I read on the Internet the more I feel resentment for what is being forced onto millions of students like me . . . LIES. There's just no way you can ask a question in a lesson. The most popular phrase from my history teacher is 'Be quiet, it's not up for debate.'"

America's Autopsy Report

To Emad -
Thank you for
your willingness to
see beyond the lies.
John Kaminski

America's Autopsy Report

The Internet Essays of John Kaminski

A Dandelion Books Publication
www.dandelionbooks.net
Tempe, Arizona

A Dandelion Books Publication
Dandelion Books, LLC
Tempe, Arizona

Library of Congress Cataloging-in-Publication Data

Kaminski, John
America's autopsy report: the internet essays of john kaminski

Library of Congress Catalog Card Number 20033104363
ISBN: 1-893302-42-3

Cover and book design by Amnet Systems Private Limited
www.amnet-systems.com

Dandelion Books, LLC
www.dandelionbooks.net

for Phillip Berrigan and Bill Cooper
and the millions of other innocent victims of
the American war machine.

Foreword

In his book *The Rise and Fall of the Third Reich*, American correspondent William Shirer described the power of a controlled media.

"I myself was to experience how easily one is taken in by a lying and censored press and radio in a totalitarian state," Shirer wrote. "Though unlike most Germans I had a daily access to foreign newspapers . . . and foreign broadcasts, my job necessitated the spending of many hours a day in combing the German press, checking the German radio, conferring with Nazi officials and going to party meetings. It was surprising and sometimes consternating to find that notwithstanding the opportunities I had to learn the facts and despite one's inherent distrust of what one learned from Nazi sources, a steady diet over the years of falsification and distortions made a certain impression on one's mind and often misled it. No one who has not lived for years in a totalitarian land can possibly conceive how difficult it is to escape the dread consequences of a regime's calculated and incessant propaganda."

At the beginning of the 21st Century, American media has become so consolidated that almost all the news Americans are exposed to is controlled by a handful of corporations. And those are all in lockstep when it comes to the policies and agendas of corporate globalization.

While Americans basked in the freedom and abundance of their country, the system changed almost imperceptibly from a model of a free society to an increasingly totalitarian state controlled by an elite network of corporate entities representing only the most stratospherically rich citizens. That network has locked down power with astonishing facility and has arranged the legal, political and economic systems of the country to enhance its advantage.

This same network controls the mass media, which in effect controls the culture. The largest corporations control what information the population is exposed to, its context, how it is spun, what is emphasized, what is left out, the tone, and the attitude. All of those messages are kept in check and channeled to instill the kind of culture that will best serve the ends of the corporate state.

The media complicity in an anti-democratic corporate agenda became painfully clear when an organized campaign of voter fraud in Florida became a pretext for a corrupt Supreme Court to nullify the choice of the voters and install the loser, whose brother just happened to have organized the voter fraud.

At that moment a large part of a complacent population began to wake up to the fact that the country had been hijacked by an anti-democratic oligarchy. What people thought was a free press turned out to be only an arm of the corporate state.

But even the most powerful men cannot entirely control evolution or contain the human aspiration for a free society. The same technologically driven Brave New World that has made such sophisticated population control possible has also produced the Internet, which has become a channel for free-flowing information, the lifeblood of resistance to totalitarianism.

The need for a source of information that is not controlled by the corporate elite has given rise to a true grassroots network of politically awakened people. John Kaminski is one of the most eloquent voices to have risen from that alternative media network. His writings have spread across the landscape of the Internet like wildfire.

Kaminski resonates with the abandoned majority because he sees clearly what is at the heart of their distress and he articulates it clearly, soulfully, and without pulling punches.

Kaminski's writing is not likely to be seen in established newspapers like the *New York Times*, at least not as of this writing. Most of his essays would be disqualified from the *New York Times* because Kaminski does not compromise one iota with the fantasy picture of the world that the *Times* maintains.

To write for the *Times*, one must ignore the fact that Bush stole the White House and is not a legitimate elected leader. One must play along with the whole charade and confer upon the office holder the dignity of the office, even if he blatantly stole it in front of everyone.

To participate in the corporate media, one must ignore a thousand other things, an outrage a day. John Kaminski doesn't care to. Kaminski has something to say and he says it. It is a message of great urgency and something a growing number of Americans want to hear. That's why his essays have been picked up enthusiastically and circulated around the Net.

In the current upheaval no one can predict with the slightest confidence where things are headed. In two more years the world will probably have changed again as much as it has since Bush took office. The direction of that change is still unclear.

In many ways the Bush administration is counter-historical. Though it now has tremendous force at its disposal, it may, like the Thousand Year Reich, be destroyed by its own pathological excesses. It is likely to fall prey to the same forces that took apart the Soviet empire when freedom of information invaded the controlled society.

But the cabal is betting on massive force to whip the world into control. The shadow government knows the biggest danger for it lies in the awakening of awareness in the American people. So it has saved its most powerful counter revolutionary measures for The Homeland.

With the Patriot Act, the administration now has the legal power to suspend all Constitutional Rights and take anyone it wants and do virtually whatever it wants with him or her. And legislation is now being written that will take the government's totalitarian powers even further. As anti-war sentiment rises, the government is ready to clamp down with a variety of repressive measures it has prepared.

Whether the people will rise up and renounce the tyranny remains to be seen. History would suggest that the U.S., like the

U.S.S.R. before it, will not be able to fully control the information flow in the country. As the oligarchy continues to escalate its war on the poor, resistance inevitably will rise. And the flow of free information may make it impossible for the government to hide as much of its misdeeds as it has in the past.

In two years, the *Times* may have been forced to change so much that work like John Kaminski's will be deemed "fit to print" by the Paper of Record. The ideas that would disqualify Kaminski's work from the *Times* today may no longer be possible to suppress. John's writing is part of the awakening of America to its own inherent democratic power.

In a future, more enlightened *New York Times*, you may read Kaminski. But you can read Kaminski's work today in this book. His new and archival material appears in many places on the Web, such as Rense.com. Read it and breathe deeply of it. You are going to need it.

David Cogswell
Author of *Chomsky For Beginners*,
Publisher of *Headblast* (davidcogswell.com).

Introduction

What follows is a kind of diary of the year 2002 by an aging American male who was profoundly affected by the horror of the events of September 11, 2001. The straightforward nature of the tragedy—mass death and mourning—was not what had the profound effect. Because fifteen minutes after the attacks happened, I knew this was no straightforward event. I knew that thousands of American lives had been preposterously sacrificed on the evil altar of political intrigue.

Those people who jumped from the tops of skyscrapers or were buried under thousands of tons of cement were not victims of an assault by foreign terrorists; they were collateral damage garbage of the aspirations of men whom we have seen on television, who speak words of utter contempt disguised as concern for their fellow humans, and whose day of reckoning is coming in the seismic revelations of future history.

These commentaries were written for and published on a group of courageous websites, notably rense.com, scoop.co.nz in New Zealand, and bluegreenearth.com in Ireland. Many also have appeared on the American Patriot Friends Network, paranoia.com, serendipity.com, flybynews.com, Lewis News, Online Journal, questionsquestions.com, What Really Happened, various Indymedia sites, Information Clearinghouse, Censor This 1, democrats.com, unknownnews.net, viewzone.com, falloutshelternews.com, propagandamatrix.com, Retort Magazine, Ellis C. Taylor's Looking into the Dark Places, the Baltimore Chronicle, CCW on Target, the Hamiltonian, Global Circle Net, radicalpress.com, libertypost.net and whoseflorida.com, as well as print media Paranoia magazine, The Idaho Observer, Z magazine and the Country Chronical of Enfield, NH.

Special thanks to Jeff Rense, David Marvasti of timewedo.com, David Cogswell of headblast.com, and Paul Fearon of worldnewsstand.net for running my essays in special groupings.

John Kaminski
Englewood, Florida, USA
February 2003

Contents

1

No one is safe from America's killer president

Now, no one is safe from America's killer president.

The Senate's passage of the ludicrously misnamed Homeland Security bill is easily the biggest bad joke in American history, because in declaring war on all peoples of the world—including its own citizens—it presages a new Dark Age in world history, one in which the United States may annihilate any other country for any reason it concocts, or for no reason at all. The bill is ludicrously misnamed because nothing in this nation's history has ever jeopardized its citizens' security to this degree.

Most tragic of all, however, is the complete destruction of that beacon of hope for the whole world for two centuries, the U.S. Constitution. Completely gone are the right to a fair trial, the right to be safe in one's home, the right to confront one's accuser, the right to legal representation and the right to be recognized as innocent until proven guilty in a court of law.

Now, America simply kills mere suspects from the air with unmanned planes, or throws them into jail without possibility of trial, arbitrarily decreed guilty by biased political functionaries and executed with no chance to prove one's innocence. And further, Attorney General John Ashcroft plans further incursions into

America's privacy by placing new restrictions on Internet and phone communications.

Though surely few in Congress realize it yet, America's legislators essentially voted themselves out of existence by passing the bill, because now the majority of governmental security functions are lumped together under the arbitrary aegis of Homeland Security, bypassing Congress with its decision-making controlled directly by the president and his unconfirmed henchman, the director of Homeland Security.

Congress, as it has been for many years, is now merely window-dressing for the criminal charades of the dictator, which is exactly what happened to the Roman republic all those long years ago.

Congress has approved the mass killing of many American citizens by passing the Homeland Security Act by shamefully wide margins in both the House and the Senate. A minor provision in the legislation gives absolute authority to nonmedical administrative personnel to mandate dangerous, untested vaccinations for all American citizens.

Since so many American military personnel died from receiving untested and mysterious vaccinations prior to the first Gulf War, and since vaccine stores presumably to be used in mass vaccinations are either out-of-date or untested, many fatalities are expected from these dangerous inoculations. Most conscientious doctors have advocated refusing the shots, but the legislation provides for arrest (and possible confiscation of property) of those refusing to accept "legally" ordered vaccinations.

Adding a provision that protects manufacturers of the ingredients from malpractice lawsuits in the event of death or infirmity is another sardonic insult included in the legislation. And investigating the real owners of the companies who are about to foist these injurious substances on ignorant Americans reveals them to be insiders of the highest echelon, some with direct ties to the president's father.

In addition, medical opinion reveals this whole issue to be a complete, cynical, financial boondoggle. The Centers for Disease Control has announced the new smallpox vaccine is not to be recommended for HIV people, anyone on immunosuppressive drugs, or anyone with eczema. The CDC quoted a new study in the *Journal of Allergy and Clinical Immunology* describing reactions that include blindness, scarring, and death. So the vaccine is therefore contraindicated in all these cases, according to the CDC.

Following is a quote from the internet website, http://www.thedoctorwithin.com/articles/smallpox.html:

> Eczema patients alone comprise half the US population. AIDS patients and those on immunosuppressive drugs add another significant proportion to the group of those who shouldn't be vaccinated.
>
> In addition, the omniscient media seem to have forgotten that most Americans over 31 years of age have already been vaccinated for smallpox, since the vaccine was only halted in 1971 in the US. Remember? So if the vaccine is supposed to work, then obviously these people will not need a new shot, right?
>
> Then who does that leave? Ten percent of the population would be a reasonable estimate.
>
> It's not much of a stretch to see how the threat of smallpox is a marketing tool, right out of classic Bernay's Public Relations 101, that is being used to justify paying vaccine manufacturers $800 million for a vaccine that is unproven, untested, and contraindicated for 90% of the population.
>
> Why then are our new masters shrieking about the 280 million doses we need to protect the American people from this imminent bioterrorist threat?
>
> Could it just be the money?

In addition, it's well known in history that smallpox vaccinations in 19th century England caused cases of smallpox to skyrocket, from around 2,000 before vaccinations started to around 80,000 afterwards, which is why most European countries stopped vaccinating then and still don't to this day. Yet our completely untrustworthy Senate approved this measure by a vote of 90–9, approved certain jeopardy for the collective health of the American people simply for hefty campaign contributions from drug companies.

What's important to notice is that smallpox vaccination in the U.S. persisted another 30 years after the disease was at an incidence of practically zero. Again, the only source of death from smallpox in the U.S. for 30 years was from the vaccine itself. [(Mendelsohn, *World Book*. 1994, p.232 vol. 24, 25) See thedoctorwithin, above].

It's difficult to discern which element of the Homeland Security legislation is actually the worst encroachment on the rapidly eroding independence of America's citizenry. One which has sparked much complaint is the removal of civil service protections for Homeland Security employees, to improve security aspects of America's "war on terror," according to President Bush. This assault of the well-being of American workers nullifies 70 years of battling for justice in the workplace. Another insulting aspect of the bill is a boondoggle "institute" at a Texas university near the president's ranch.

One glaring affront to hardworking Americans was a provision allowing companies that left the country to avoid federal taxes (think the Enron, Halliburton and Harken models) to be eligible for Homeland Security contracts. This is clearly a sop to the president's close friends, who do business in this exact manner. If the United States had an actual attorney general, he would have long ago investigated these criminal cheaters. John Ashcroft only persecutes those who threaten the profits of the American elite, as the moldering, sabotaged probes into both the 9/11 horror and the anthrax murders clearly indicate.

We desperately need an attorney general who will enforce the laws of the land and protect people, not this insane Pentacostal functionary whose sole purpose seems to be to assist in the destruction of all Constitutional protections for average citizens.

Apart from these treasonous intrusions into the lives of ordinary people lurks America's new penchant for starting wars in various areas of the world for purposes that are kept hidden from the general public.

The American mass murder in Afghanistan was ostensibly aimed at bringing to justice the alleged perpetrators of the 9/11 disasters in New York City and Washington. The aim of this mission failed and was forgotten.

Now Afghanistan has degenerated into sheer murderous anarchy, drug-smuggling chaos, and death from residual radioactivity, all conveniently overlooked by the world's major newspapers, or consigned to the back pages.

It is important to remember that this is what other countries in the world should look forward to experiencing after the U.S. decides its "war on terror" should cross their borders. What is happening in Afghanistan is what will happen in Iraq, followed by what will happen to other countries on the immediate U.S. hit list. What will be left of the world after that hit list is accomplished? Nothing but misery, rubble, and heaps of innocent corpses, sanctified as the new American export.

And as the current Iraq saga meanders toward a new criminal conclusion, what are we to think of a world of spineless bureaucrats (including our own CIA), who for months protested that President Bush was clearly lying about his reasons to invade that desperate country, but eventually knuckled under to American pressure (read: were bribed into accepting) and joined the sick parade of "democratic" nations ready to once again sacrifice the Iraqi people for the sins of the Zionist petronazis.

In a country known around the world for the power of its democratic institutions to temper dictatorial impulses of its previous leaders, Homeland Security stands as a colossal betrayal of the peoples of the world, because it means that all of the lectures given by America over the years that democracy was the best way to govern are now exposed as cynical lies, convenient ruses used by American corporate shills to bleed other countries dry of their natural resources.

Democracy in the United States clearly no longer works, evidenced by the fact that the opposition party—the Democrats, which crafted most of the Homeland Security bill—no longer opposes in any significant way the expansionist aims of its unelected, undemocratic dictator.

President George W. Bush is remarkable among American presidents for his distinctive lack of business and life achievements prior to assuming his office in Washington. All of his business enterprises were devious shell corporations sustained by his father's super-rich friends. And now we have a government of just such a nature.

In addition, the second president Bush has "distinguished" himself for his record of allowing executions of mentally ill persons in Texas to prove his toughness about "law and order." Now innocent American people—as well as people all over the world—are about to learn what the people of Afghanistan have so recently and tragically learned: that no life is sacred if it stands in the way of schemes by the power elite to suck billions of dollars from a tottering economy.

Now, no one is safe from America's executioner *par excellence.*

Just ask Paul Wellstone.

2

Dreaming of love in blooms of fire

For all souls lost on September 11, 2001

My recurring dream awakens into flame, engulfing fire destroying a large city—always the same scene, a Manchester in England or a Munich firebombed in Germany, consumed by raging sworls of mint green and orange, majestically devouring shadowy landscapes in wind-whipped sheets of overwhelming flame, and the small hints of muted figures, silently screaming silhouettes, randomly running, gesticulating briefly, hysterically, before disappearing from the scene forever.

Or that famous elk, silhouetted by the flaming forest, caught in the glow of the river, forever. And always the sense of people I know well caught in the shadow of the flames who will not be seen again. Our soldiers. Our children. Our grandfathers. How we will miss them.

At first I thought, how precious, how inestimably valuable, these visions of fire, distilled from news reports of tragedy and war, ambush and atrocity, scrambled and shuffled by a bedraggled brain that clings to life, the fire and its dream lessons no less than the instantaneous summing up of our existences, lives of labor and leisure, of want and woe, suddenly snuffed in a hard rain of violent heat, with no recourse to postscript and second-guessing, just gone, people gone, memories no longer operative. Such is my memory of September 11, 2001, a rain of fire and little silhouettes running into oblivion, or falling from the sky, followed by cloth patches from some VFW post floating down a small rivulet of muddy water by the side of some road I have never traveled.

But the flame show keeps running. The fire in my dreams does not go out. It can be run back over and over, so that the sense of loss, the picture of destruction, runs continuously, like some vapor trail of desire seeking analysis of motive, dissection of purpose, some kind of fetid sweetness in mint green death. I fancy certain scenes are filmclips stored in the library of my moviehouse, with inane slugs that read like website names—swipnet or poleclips—to be summoned into vision when the cold engine of my dreams revs up around 4 AM each morning. These filmclips of flame that would be precious memories of sacrifice never quite go away, and events that are so serious to each of us become so boring to all of us. Ho hum, life and death. Who was that person who saved our lives, and was it that important?

There are voices, not quite audible but unmistakable, uttering urgent instructions, vital warnings, to shadows running through high tides of orange death. Pictures of actions that speak of incomprehensible sacrifice, where the last thing you have to give becomes the first thing that comes to mind. And always the final panoply of red to black, where all things go thin and gray and descriptions become mercifully partial as the reality you wish to describe becomes just too grim. Loss is, after all, statistical. First the thing is there, then it's not.

And when it's not, when the thing is certifiably gone, then I dream of the flames, mint green and orange, people I would have liked lost in a fog of pain, watching their arms melt, their hopes vaporizing in a holocaust that was not of their control, that was not their duty to overcome, that was totally unexpected in the moment of giant sheets of flaming rain. And from this terrible pastiche of misery and deceit have we become who we are, dreaming of love in blooms of fire.

Would that people fell from the sky only in dreams.

3

Brainwashington

Be clear about what you know. About the markers that trigger responses in your own brain. About the boundaries of your own reality.

You are an American, most likely. Put your hand over your heart and close your eyes. Remember your childhood, that high school football game. How proud you were, how safe you felt. This was in the days, most likely, before you knew that Charles Calley and Bob Kerrey had put bullets through the brains of little Vietnamese children. Calley and Kerrey. One went to a cushy prison and was respected by generals. The other was given medals, elected governor and senator, allowed to run for president. And when he tried to tell everyone he killed women and children, no one wanted to listen. We all wanted him to keep his medals.

Put your hand over your heart. Watch that flag wave, and feel the joy. Feel the joy of putting a bullet through the head of a little Vietnamese child. It is the American way. Then covered up in the American way. Metamorphosed by blithering sycophantic media into patriotism over fictional events, events created by the very people who pretend to be attacked. We pretend we are not killers. We pretend we are patriots, and kill the rest of the world for their obstinacy over not believing the fictions we have created for our own amusement, for our own profit.

The best slaves are those who believe they are free.

Understand the phrase: Americans are victims of the largest media brainwashing campaign in history. Realize that Eisenhower and MacArthur, two of America's most esteemed generals, killed American veterans who came to Washington to collect back pay they had been promised. Realize our president's grandfather profited from investments in the government of Adolf Hitler (go ahead—ask me for this reference, and I'll give you ten); realize our current president made all of his money from crooked stock deals and phony oil deals, many of which were bankrolled by the bin Ladin family of Saudi Arabia. George W. Bush's grandfather was a Nazi sympathizer who actually was censured by the U.S. government for just that behavior; George W. Bush's father works hand-in-hand with the same Saudi royalty that funnels money to terrorists whose only aim is to provide an excuse for lavish expenditures on U.S. military adventures, and the Bushes and the Saudis profit from the use of weapons which they provide to destroy fictional threats they themselves have created for the very purpose of making money and hiding the scam behind the veil of pompous patriotism.

This is how Americans have been brainwashed.

We believe we live in a free country. Fifty-first in the world in health care. Somewhere in the 20s in environmental awareness.

Our media doesn't report these things, because our media is owned by the same people who are starting all the wars, downing all the airplanes, and then conducting in-depth investigations and not telling anyone what they find.

What's the total number of people who saw those two missiles hit Flight 800? Over 700. Or the documentation by engineers about the structural damage in Oklahoma City? At least three bombs, maybe five?

If the invasion of Afghanistan was to capture the perpetrators of the World Trade Center destruction, how come they weren't captured? If the U.S. government could name all 22 hijackers two days after the attacks, why is there no more information on them and their superiors three months later?

Most intelligent people believe the attacks on the World Trade Center and the Pentagon were conceived and directed by people inside the United States, not by people living in caves in Afghanistan.

Why is the new leader of Afghanistan the same guy who was conducting the negotiations with the oil giant Unocal for a pipeline well before the attacks?

Why were FEMA personnel in New York City the night before the attacks?

Why didn't U.S. defenses shoot down that plane that hit the Pentagon? They had an hour and 20 minutes to do it, and fighter jets to do the job only ten minutes away.

Why do you still believe what you hear on TV more than what you are reading here?

And why are people getting excited over some meaningless vote in Congress about political money? No stupid bill is going to change the way things are.

Why isn't Ken Lay in jail for stealing millions from ordinary people? Why doesn't our president care more about ordinary citizens than he does his rich friends? And why does anybody support a president like that? Unless they're lying crooks themselves.

Why has nobody ever heard of al-Qaeda before now? Did the U.S. CIA invent them for this particular occasion?

Why did all the events that came after Sept. 11—the suspension of the Bill of Rights, the invasion of Afghanistan—fulfill plans that the powers that be had expressly wished for before Sept. 11? Why doesn't anyone find that suspicious? Laughably fraudulent!

How stupid are the American people not to know that the fix is in?

Now Bush and Powell and Rumsfeld are talking about bombing many other countries around the world: Iraq, North Korea, Iran, Somalia, Venezuela, Colombia. What do we do when megalomaniacal criminals like Bush and friends are the law, and we are its hapless victims?

We are brainwashed, apparently with no hope of remedy, certainly not from those who seek to fine-tune the "system"; we have never seen a candidate who even recognizes the problem, or, not since Henry George anyway.

Be clear about what you know. By not acting against the insane warmongers, you are participating in the destruction of civilization. Helping us lose our freedoms, what's left of them.

Remember this: waving the flag means putting a bullet in the brain of a child so some rich person can make more money. This is the freedom we strive to maintain.

4

Morphing into reasonlessness

I "do the wire" at the local paper (or I did until they fired me), which in media parlance means I select the stories, devise the headlines, choose the photographs and pretty much determine the topical information you ingest with your morning coffee, at least insofar as the wider world is concerned as seen from this particular neighborhood. Your world, national and state news is what I gather, write the headlines for, choosing the accompanying photographs and displaying them all on several—up to a dozen or so—printed pages every night. The purely "local" news is compiled by another department; it's not my bailiwick.

I go fast; that is to say, I scan a large pool of information, determine what I think is important, and paste it onto a number of computerized pages. Speed is necessary, as are snap judgments and reflexive instincts because of the large number of words (and small size of type) required to fill that amount of space.

The process is not unlike quiltmaking, I would guess, with similar rhythms of patternings and types of stitching. I make a picture for you to read and thereby know about the world. It's editing and journalism, two time-honored professions.

As far back as I could imagine it, I would be a kind of town crier, only now in an anonymous and sped up cyber age, though I guess town criers have always been anonymous.

Anyway, the point of this note, this spontaneous reckoning and recapitulation at this particular uneventful moment in time, is that just now in a dream—a medication-induced, sore back wreck of a mattress tinged, repetitive hallucination of early morning—I have perceived the true pattern of my news gathering, how it's done and what it means, and how very far from useful it all is.

The dream was a record (in this day and age, you might call it a CD), playing over and over again, containing certain songs, perhaps with words, perhaps not, each song fulfilling a certain need or requirement, each song possessing lyrics that could not quite be distinguished, although all seemed familiar—if not important or amusing.

I became aware that the record was playing over and over, so that in the subsequent playings, the memory of the songs became fresher, the understanding of them more developed. What I was doing in this dream was not clear to me: it seemed I was walking through a mall, halfheartedly glancing through plate glass windows at the numbing variety of consumer goods, and the songs that were playing at first simply accompanied me on my walk, but later began to take control of my thinking. Especially as they played for the third or fourth times. Think too much Dionne Warwick and a bursting desire to slam a radio into a million pieces.

Then it dawned on me that the radio was not playing songs at all, it was playing cybernetic patterns that fit into my expectations, formulaic messages that plugged into a certain sequence of the reasoning of the way I viewed the world. Then it began to become obvious that the songs contained no words, only sounds that at first appeared to be words, sounds that I expected to be words, but which were really not when I listened intently. They were not words; they were patterns of expectation. I was hearing what I wanted to hear, what I had chosen to hear, in the way I had chosen to hear it. And soon, on about the sixth or seventh playing of them, they became completely different, and virtually interchangeable. One song, though different, was the same as another; and each of them plugged into my expectations.

Which takes us back to my news gathering, as I put a pot of coffee on the cooker and get out of bed to write this down. What I construct for you each morning—and more to the point, what is provided for me by the Associated Press (a typical, established, corporate newsgathering entity) to construct for you each morning—is a picture of the world that has been constructed by someone else for a specific purpose. What that purpose actually is . . . is more a matter for your own conjecture rather than for my analysis of it. After all, I provide you with the news; you must interpret it for yourself.

All of which is to say . . . be aware of what you're hearing. The songs are mostly the same, and more important, often do not contain any real information. I think many times these songs and stories and words simply try to be a representation of what other people think you would like to hear.

The words, if you listen very carefully to them and perhaps more than once or twice, are not really words at all. The same words over and over again become not words but emotional triggers (try "homeland security") to get you to behave in a certain way, to think certain things in a way they would like you to think them, or, all too often, to get you not to think at all. They are merely plug-ins to buzz you in a certain way to get you to do certain things. What that way is, and what those things are, are up to you to find out.

5

Think first, mourn later

September 11, 2002

Whether they were genuinely the desperate acts of disgruntled foreign terrorists or the cynical, murderous ploys of high-level agents provocateur, the events of 9/11/2001 were a consequence of America's thoughtless, oppressive and often murderous foreign policy.

Be clear about this: we don't know who planned these acts, because adequate investigations have been thwarted at every turn by the highest levels of the American government. That in itself says a great deal. But either way, whether the plan supposedly constructed in a cell of hairy malcontents in Hamburg, Germany was actually generated from a high-tech cavern in Afghanistan or a boring conference room in Langley, Virginia, the result was the same, and the blame is the same: American foreign policy inflicted this great wound on the American people.

Our unwillingness to come to grips with this painful realization guarantees that we will suffer more tragedies of this type and magnitude in the future, because we simply refuse to see the light. We simply refuse to admit our guilty sins of indifference and not really caring about what happens to other people. We refuse to admit that we don't mind killing a few people if we're going to be financially rewarded for it. Think lower gas prices.

Today we reopen this great wound one year after truly evil deeds were perpetrated upon humanity. Great as the pain may be, reopening this wound must not be a cause to stop thinking, both about the true motivations for the attacks and the inconsistencies in subsequent explanations. Because to shroud ourselves in pseudo-patriotism and rely on steadfast solidarity will simply not get the job done if we are ever to find out why this happened.

We need to ask questions that are very hard to ask.

Why, with so much time between knowledge of the hijackings and the time of impact, were these planes not intercepted by the greatest military defense force in the world? Especially the Pentagon plane, which crashed 45 minutes AFTER the first plane in New York. Why did NORAD not immediately scramble fighter jets when it learned the first plane had been hijacked? One year later, we have had no satisfactory answer to this question.

Why did our president say, on two different occasions, that he saw the first plane strike the World Trade Center when it was not televised?

And why did he keep reading a meaningless story to schoolchildren when he knew both towers had been hit? When he knew the nation was under attack. What was he trying to prove? That he didn't know?

Why have we never seen a single picture of the plane that supposedly hit the Pentagon?

Why was the invasion of Afghanistan, which had been planned earlier in the summer, called a retaliation for the terrorist attacks if it already had been planned?

Why, in subsequent analyses, is it now obvious that numerous warnings forwarded from Russia, Israel, Egypt and many other intelligence services were ignored or disregarded by American security forces? Did somebody in the highest levels of the American government want this to happen? Why were there deliberate cover-ups of clues by the FBI?

Why was the Patriot Act passed so quickly? Why didn't more people point out that this act absolutely trashed our Constitution? And why did so many of our elected representatives sign this bill without even reading it? In my opinion, the Patriot Act was passed so the government could prevent information from participants in its own plot to be revealed to the public, which is why all these trials of so-called terror suspects need to be completely public, lest certain government criminals get away with their dirty deeds.

What are we fighting for if the Constitution is no longer in force? What country are we living in?

Why did someone call San Francisco Mayor Willie Brown and tell him not to fly on September 11?

Why were so many employees of the World Trade Center not at their desks that morning?

Why did a Brooklyn student tell his friends in the weeks before that in a few weeks, those towers would be gone?

Why did a South Carolina National Guardsman recount a story from July that his superiors told him there would be a military exercise in September that they would all have to be ready for?

Why does President Bush insist he had no prior knowledge when there is so much evidence to the contrary?

Why don't newspapers and TV commentators talk about the longstanding relationship of the Bush and bin Ladin families? Or the ties to Adolf Hitler of the president's grandfather, Prescott Bush, in the early 1940s?

Why was the bin Ladin family flown out of the country when all planes in the country were grounded?

Why did the American government have the names of all the hijackers two days after the attacks but has had virtually no new intelligence since?

Why was Atta's passport found in the street near the World Trade Center, or another hijacker's Qu'ran found left in a parked car at Logan Airport?

Why doesn't President Bush admit that Americans financed Saddam Hussein, al-Qaeda and Osama bin Laden as allies to build them up to the point where they could become suitable enemies, much in the same way that Ford and Rockefeller sent money to the Bolsheviks and Hitler earlier in the last century?

Why did the World Trade Center towers collapse the way they did, with perfect symmetry, as if demolished? Why did three World Trade Center buildings collapse, when only two were hit by jetliners?

Why was molten steel found glowing weeks after the attacks at the bottoms of all three? And why were the biggest seismic spikes in the area at the time recorded BEFORE the buildings actually fell to the ground?

These are all signs, clues, portents, that potentially indicate a false story has been told.

And there are hundreds more questions like this, ranging from possible remote control of the airliners, that questionable fate of the plane that crashed in Pennsylvania, Taliban fighters escaping Afghanistan in a U.S. airlift . . . on and on. The only thing now certain about the attacks of 9/11/2001 is that American public officials have lied not only about the events themselves but about their responses to those events.

One thing certainly untrue was the statement of George W. Bush that the attacks happened because terrorists hate our freedom. If the foreign terrorist motivation is actually true, they didn't attack because they hate our freedom; they attacked because they hate the things that America is doing to their freedom, most notably, support for anti-democratic dictatorships in Saudi Arabia and Pakistan.

And if the insider, U.S. government connection turns out to be true, this is still a consequence of our own misguided, murderous foreign policy, only with 3,000-plus Americans caught in the crossfire and blown to bits as a sacrifice to a small minority of well-connected bigots who wanted to—and have—turned America into a full-blown police state.

On this first anniversary of the tragedies, now is not the time to mourn; now is the time to think, and ask questions. This is what all those dead people would want us to do, and God help us if their deaths were in vain, as so many people in power want them to be.

Don't let their deaths be in vain. We need to expose this beast that threatens us all.

6

The tide of lies keeps rising

Maybe it has always been this way.

Phony pretexts—repeated often enough—eventually become real reasons in the public's lazy mind. Things that we know for certain are not true become true in the echo chamber of media sound bites simply through endless repetition.

Iraq has weapons of mass destruction. Former weapons inspector Scott Ritter, a card-carrying Republican who voted for Bush, debunked that hysterical assertion months ago; yet the Bush administration fanatics carry on with their murderous mantra: "Iraq has weapons of mass destruction," and eventually, the whole world falls into line, repeating the phrase as if in a hypnotic trance. It is the formula devised by the Nazi deity Adolf Hitler: Invent the lie and repeat it often enough and it becomes the truth, no matter what the facts actually are.

True—this is not exactly a new thing. Nor does false propaganda arise from just one side of the political spectrum. Our newest Nobel Peace Prize winner, former President Jimmy Carter, once canceled U.S. participation in the Olympic Games because of Soviet aggression in Afghanistan. But recently we have learned that Carter's top foreign policy adviser, Zbigniew Brzezinski, admitted starting that fight and creating the conditions that lured the Soviets to attach themselves to that toxic tar baby. Many Americans complained at the time about how many athletic careers were betrayed by the withdrawal from the Olympics, but I tend to think of how many people were needlessly killed by what was essentially a capricious political intrigue, although it did eventually lead to the breakup of the Soviet megastate.

Perhaps the quintessential phony pretext was Hitler's 1934 use of a fire in Germany's Reichstag building, which he insisted was a crime perpetrated by Communists, but most historians theorize was a ruse used to institute new repressive measures throughout Nazi Germany. Many people theorize that the destruction wreaked on Sept. 11, 2001 in the United States was an event belonging in the same category, a false terror incident used to implement more repressive measures in the U.S. as well as serve as a bogus justification for murderous, hideous target practice in hapless Afghanistan. As the Bush administration continues to block numerous inquiries into relevant aspects of that tortuous day, the suspicion grows that he and his petronazi cabal arranged and supervised those horrible attacks.

The Vietnam war, which cost the world some 3 million lives, is now largely believed to have been started by just such a phony pretext: the infamous Gulf of Tonkin incident, which initially was reported as a minor attack on an American ship off the coast of Hanoi but now is consensually regarded as a total fabrication by American warmongers. The similarity to what is happening now in regard to Iraq is eerily familiar.

And the events leading up to this present day—when the U.S. is perched to strike with its finger on the trigger of its massive war machine—give even more credence to the suspicion that claims about Iraq's aggressive nature are just a smokescreen with multiple purposes.

The first deception is of course the amount of oil beneath the ground of that country, second in quantity in the world only to Saudi Arabia. It would certainly help the disintegrating American economy to suddenly be in control of a huge new source of oil, for which we could then name our own price.

The second deception is the creation of a U.S. staging area for eventual military control of that whole oil-producing region. With our foreign policy sadly reflecting Israel's genocidal intent to carve out a much larger area of control for itself, the U.S. would undoubtedly pick fights with Iran, Pakistan, Syria, Libya and even Saudi Arabia and Egypt, just like America has arbitrarily picked this current fight with Iraq, simply because the bully is large enough and there is no country, nor coalition of countries, tough enough to resist it.

The third deception is that we are doing this for the welfare of the American people, who surely will not profit from a windfall cache of cheap oil (the profits will be kept by the corporate titans), and who surely will suffer from sending troops into an area poisoned by expended radioactive ordnance. Even the American troops themselves have been poisoned by supposedly preventive inoculations which contain ingredients whose purpose the government will not reveal. What benefit will Americans get from this? None. Only more insoluble tragedy.

But it is the fourth deception that is the most egregious of all, and provides the key to all those other deceptions perpetrated in the name of American dominance. Ten weeks ago, Saddam Hussein was off the radar screen, a minor Middle Eastern despot kept in check by sadistic sanctions and random bombings that have taken a heavy toll over the past decade without serious objection by the so-called civilized world. Then came the new round of lies. A meeting in Czechoslovakia, long since debunked, alleged a terror connection between al-Qaeda and Iraq. Then an endless succession of unprovable claims from the White House, repeated with increasing frequency until they became the consensus truth in the world's brainwashing, corporate media.

The use of the supposed threat from Saddam Hussein is directly connected to—and meant to deflect scrutiny from—the Bush cabal's attempt to block legitimate inquiries into the World Trade Center slaughter and the corporate thievery of Enron, Halliburton, and Harken corporations. If we're writing about aspects of Iraq, we can't be writing about Vice President Cheney's illegal refusal to reveal how he tilted America's energy regulations to benefit the corporate plunderers he represents.

Now we are going to war, to kill and maim thousands, and to poison even many of our own finest young people, just in order to keep embarrassing questions from being asked of the rogue aristocrats who have hijacked American democracy and turned it all into their own Ku Klux Klan version of corporate truth. There is no politician in America powerful enough or brave enough to oppose this atrocity. The ugly American people remain cowered by fear in their own financial self-centeredness, unable to confront the genuine truth of the matter: that American leaders of both parties have worked to cover up the murders of thousands of their own people, and countless more thousands around the world, and no one of any consequential reputation has the guts to stand up and say so.

And through it all, the tide of lies keeps rising. What will become of us?

7

Why your vote won't matter

This essay was written a week before the November 5, 2002 elections

So, you're going to cast your vote to prove that you live in a democracy, are you? Guess again, Chuck.

Your vote does not matter. It might not even be counted, assuming you're allowed to vote to begin with. In fact, if you're black, and the first four letters of your last name match the first four letters on that famously fabricated list of Florida felons, you definitely won't be voting at all, because the state of Florida hasn't bothered to fix its mistakes from the last election—the same problems that allowed George W. Bush to slither into the White House like the rapine reptilian he is are still in force.

Plus, the thoughtful Republicans in Florida, led by the president's porcine brother Jeb, have added some new obstacles to counting the votes accurately, the best of which is the new touch-screen voting system, which eliminates the paper trail that would expose ballot manipulation and also would be used for legitimate recounts in the case of very close elections. No more recounts—isn't that efficient?

Angry columnist Jackson Thoreau recently penned a comprehensive roundup of Republican shenanigans going on around the country to reduce the Democratic vote. Read the whole story at http://www.americaheldhostile.com/ed110102.shtml or let me give you this brief synopsis.

You have to hand it to the Republicans for evil inventiveness. In New Mexico, the GOP tried to bribe the Green Party to run candidates in three Congressional races to siphon votes away from popular Democrats.

Of course, the principled Greens refused. In Michigan, Republicans recruited nine "stealth" candidates to run as Democrats, thereby discouraging legitimate opposition. In early voting in Dallas, Texas, voting machines were recording Democratic votes as Republican; the GOP, when caught, blamed it on "miscalibration." In Arkansas, many African American voters were asked to produce their voter ID cards in a blatant effort at intimidation. Officials in South Dakota are demanding new restrictions on Native American voters.

Did you know that Republicans used private planes from Enron Corp. and Halliburton Co., the firm headed by Dick Cheney that also practiced phony accounting fraud, to crisscross the state and block the counting of Florida votes? This time around in the Florida primary, misleading fliers were circulated again, saying that some people should vote on a day after Nov. 5. Similar fliers were circulated in Florida before the 2000 election, which some say confused some voters there. I bet they'd like to hire Arthur Andersen to audit Florida's elections system.

But these are trivial gestures—distracting parlor games, really—and not the real issue that proves your own vote will not matter.

President Bush supposedly signed new Election Reform Legislation into law earlier this month. Kay J. Maxwell, president of the League of Women Voters of the United States, stated: "Because of the hard work of many? elected officials, advocacy groups, and grassroots organizations such as ours, America's voters can look forward to real changes at their polling places over the next few years." Right, the next few years. But not this year. Nothing, especially in Florida, has really changed at all.

Where we begin to get a little closer to the truth is not in the debate about who can vote, although that certainly is important, but in the mechanics of the voting. Call it the hanging chad tangent, if you like.

Like the voting machines. Who provides them, and who operates them? Most recently, a former Florida secretary of state profited by being a lobbyist for both the state's counties and the company that sold some of the touch-screen voting machines used in last month's botched primary election. Sandra Mortham, who served as the state's top elections official from 1995 to 1999, is a lobbyist for both Election Systems & Software and the Florida Association of Counties, which exclusively endorsed the company's touch-screen machines in return for a commission . . . Mortham received a commission from ES&S for every county that bought its touch-screen machines. The exact terms have not been disclosed . . . Mortham is of course a Republican who before a scandal brought her down was going to be Jeb Bush's running mate in Florida.

And of course, there is the current problem in Nebraska. Look at the documents, see the loop: ES&S, according to the Nebraska Elections Division, is the ONLY vote-counting company certified to sell machines in Nebraska. ES&S counts 80 percent of the votes; the remaining 20 percent are hand counts.

ES&S is owned by the McCarthy Group; Michael McCarthy runs the McCarthy Group; Michael McCarthy is the Campaign Treasurer for Republican Senator Chuck Hagel; The FEC designates Michael McCarthy as a Primary Campaign Committee for Candidate Chuck Hagel; and Chuck Hagel's financials list the McCarthy Group as an Asset, with his investment valued at $1-$5 million.

Hagel came to Omaha from Washington, where he worked with the first George Bush Administration. In news articles by the *Omaha World-Herald*, Hagel said he was coming to Omaha to become president and partner in the McCarthy Group and Chairman of American Information Systems.

In his congressional bio he is said to have come to Omaha "to prepare for running for office." The first thing he did was run American Information Systems, a vote-counting company. Hagel was the first Republican in 24 years to win a Nebraska senatorial campaign. He continues to disclose an investment of $1.5 million in the McCarthy Group, but he does not identify the underlying assets (ES&S). His disclosure documents omit any mention of American Information Systems at all. John Gottschalk has been reported as a director for both the World-Herald Company Inc. (concentrating on the non-newspaper subsidiaries) and ES&S. He was also involved with Senator Hagel in the World USO, has relationships with James Baker; he is listed as a USO pal of George W. Bush. Hmm, there's that certain odor again. (The unabridged information on this can be accessed at http://www.talion.com/election-machines.html#Nebraska.)

This is just the tip of the iceberg when it comes to voting machines, by the way, as you could read in the aforementioned reference.

Perhaps the greatest vote-fixing story of the computer age occurred in the 1988 Republican primary in New Hampshire, where it is likely that a notoriously riggable collection of "Shouptronic" computers "preordained" voting results to give George H. W. Bush his "Hail Mary" victory in New Hampshire. Nobody save a small group of computer engineers, like John Sununu, the state's Republican governor, would be the wiser.

James M. and Kenneth F. Collier wrote in their 1992 classic, *Votescam: The Stealing of America*":

> People who mistrust the voting process cannot, in the traditional American way, accept the defeat of their candidates gracefully and work loyally with the winners. Instead, more and more American voters are feeling "had," "scammed," "hoodwinked" by the voting system. Trust has almost departed. There is the nagging, unproven, yet pervasive feeling that the "experts," the "spin doctors," the "covert operators" and the "private interests" have put their technicians and consultants in absolute control of the national vote count, and that in any selected situation these computer wizards can and will program the vote as their masters wish.

"This New Hampshire primary was perhaps the most polled primary election in American history, and in the end, the Republican voters in the state confounded the predictions of nearly every published survey of voter opinion," Collier wrote. Gallup's glaring error and the miscalls of other polling organizations once again raised questions about the accuracy of polls. What nobody seriously wrote about was that the polls were usually right and that the computers were eminently "fixable." Read the whole sorry tale at http://Votescam.com/chap1.html. When you do you'll realize that not just the second Bush was an illegitimate president.

What really determines elections is who counts the votes, and who counts the votes is somebody you probably didn't know—and if you did know them, you surely wouldn't trust them to count the votes. No government agency counts the votes. And the people who count the votes, who tell you who your next president is, have no government oversight, no audit, no official you have elected watching over them.

The people who really count the votes are the media, more specifically a politically influenced cabal of minions bought and paid for by corporate tycoons who own the nation's major media outlets. These are the same people who don't think peace demonstrations are worthy of coverage, and who in the year 2000 got together and reviewed the data from Florida and then really wouldn't tell us what they found out.

They'd only say . . . Bush won, just like the Supreme Court. The highest court of the United States wouldn't let Florida recount its ballots, and the highest media of the United States wouldn't tell us what they found when they did. In case you were wondering, there is no honest official vote total from the last election, only the one "certified" by Katherine Harris.

Evan Ravitz, founder of the website vote.org, has itemized the major problems with America's manipulable election system (http://www.vote.org/fraud.htm).

"When I directed Boulder, Colorado's Voting by Phone ballot initiative campaign in 1993 I learned many unnerving things about existing voting procedures. The problems revealed in Florida are just the beginning," Ravitz wrote. Here's his list:

1. The Voter News Service (formerly News Election Service)—which supplies ALL election-eve numbers on national and Congressional races—is a private business of the TV networks,

The *New York Times*, the *Washington Post* and the Associated Press. If you ask them how they count votes and predict outcomes they say that's proprietary information! They have no web site or other public profile. And they won't tell you a thing about how they do what they do.

2. Most votes in America are counted by computer programs which are also proprietary secrets. Not even election officials are allowed to inspect these programs (the "source code") to verify their accuracy. Election officials can test the programs (using "test decks") but any clever programmer can write a program which passes tests but falsifies the election.
3. In most jurisdictions, identification for voting is on the honor system. Signatures, if taken, are not compared to your signature on file in most places unless you are "challenged" by election judges or poll watchers, a rare event, used mostly in the South against blacks. When this system started hundreds of years ago, the election judges or poll watchers knew most everyone in their precincts. In modern America, this is rarely true.
4. Mail or absentee ballots are often delivered to old addresses, and the USPS is not supposed to forward them. Whoever gets one could fill it out in the rightful voter's name. This is discussed in the document "Florida Voter Fraud Issues" from the Florida Department Of Law Enforcement. In student and other high-turnover areas, this problem is rife.
5. In states with "early" voting, there is no system to prevent people from voting early at an elections office and then also voting at their precinct. This is going on right now as we speak. (See the Dallas anecdote above.)

So, here's the deal: the people who count the votes are the same people who both predict (via the use of polls) the winners and also report on the outcomes of these elections. Do you think they have any interest in promoting their credibility by seeing their predictions verified? After all, these are private businesses.

Also, the actual owners of the Voter News Service are super-rich media barons, with intimate ties to the power structure of America, which chooses all of the major candidates for president in every election. Do you think they might be in agreement who will win before the election ever transpires?

As the Colliers wrote of the 1988 fiasco in New Hampshire, "there was no rechecking of the computerized voting machines, no inquiry into the path of the vote from the voting machines to the central tallying place, no public scrutiny of the mechanisms of the mighty peculiar vote that saved George Bush's career and leapfrogged the relatively obscure Sununu into the White House."

The media giants who reported on—and recounted—Florida's votes in the 2000 election failed to report one simple fact: that by law, ballots rejected by counting machines have to be hand-counted. This did not occur, and this was not widely reported.

If either had occurred, you know who would not be in the White House at this moment trying to make war on the entire world. If either had occurred, our Constitutional Bill of Rights would still be in force, which now, as a result of this convenient media oversight, it is not.

The same wealthy patricians who undercount the number of people who attend antiwar demonstrations, who pretend there are no political opinions in the United States except Republican and Democratic, who deride "liberals" and blithely report that Paul Wellstone's political assassination was just a mysterious accident—and that 9/11 was an attack by disenchanted Muslim terrorists . . . these are the same people who are predicting and reporting on your elections, as well as the very ones who actually count the votes and give you the totals.

Which is why your vote in Tuesday's election will most definitely not really matter.

8

When medicines are meant to kill

Hitler claimed to have gotten his inspiration for the "final solution" from the extermination of Native Americans in the U.S. For that matter the first example of germ warfare in the U.S. was in 1763 when some of the European colonists gave friendly Indians a number of blankets that had been infected with smallpox, causing many deaths.

—*Waves Forrest*
(http://www.totse.com/en/conspiracy/the_aids_conspiracy/aidsgate.html)

Have you noticed? In the mainstream corporate media, some stories are never written.

Throughout American history the media have deliberately ignored certain subjects. Two areas especially overlooked are government drug smuggling and population control by medicines. When you think about it, these two categories go together. Because previous major events in these areas have been underreported if reported at all, new developments are simply not believed by most people. They are not aware of or have refused to believe the previous stories.

One important censored area of political activity—drug smuggling by governments—remains probably the most concealed area of activity across the entire political spectrum. Because the billionaires behind it make so much money off it, they have plenty of cash left over to influence the governments that permit it and also profit from it to fund activities that legislators would never dream of attempting to fund in the public budget. Next to the British Opium Wars in China in the 19th century, the Iran-Contra scandal of the Reagan era remains the most famous example of this, thanks to Gary Webb's Dark Alliance series which ran in the *San Jose Mercury News* before the newspaper's corporate parent pulled the story and disavowed all aspects of Webb's work.

All too often, the men making money off the behind-the-scenes drug smuggling are the same men who own the media, or are political allies of them. Currently the U.S. government conducts massive drug-smuggling operations from both Colombia and Afghanistan, the sites of two continuing "wars," the real purposes of which are not to eradicate drugs but to control their worldwide distribution. This, of course, is not reported by the newspapers of the rich.

A second significant and unreported area of the political spectrum involves medicine, specifically projects ostensibly created to improve people's health, but on a subterranean level, apparently devised with exactly the opposite intent.

An examination of these sordid examples is now critically important for all the peoples of the world, and especially Americans, since the new Homeland Security legislation, being signed by President Bush as I write this, authorizes the U.S. government to mandate certain vaccinations for American citizens that may not be refused, under penalty of law. Roll it over in your mind: vaccinations that may not be refused!

This new legislation, in effect, allows the U.S. government to conduct a campaign of mass murder against its own most vulnerable citizens, even as most Americans remain unaware of the true purpose of these diabolical pharmaceutical programs. One day they'll probably call it "population improvement."

To better understand what is actually happening with the new public relations scares involving smallpox, anthrax and other diseases as yet unnamed, a review of the recent history of U.S. immunization programs, both for what they claimed to be and what they actually accomplished in the real world, can be very instructive.

The most infamous of all these sorry chapters was uncovered shortly after the beginning of the AIDS epidemic in the 1980s. Mainstream media took their corrupt cue from the U.S. government and blamed it all on a monkey. But to skeptical medical professionals, the cover story was ludicrous, even though it's the one the public continues to accept.

In 1987, the World Health Organization was publicly accused of unleashing the AIDS epidemic in central Africa, as a result of its smallpox vaccine programs. The most logical explanation to account for the millions of Africans infected is that the vaccines used in the WHO mass inoculation programs were contaminated.

The AIDS medical establishment unquestioningly parrots the notion that a black African heterosexual AIDS epidemic transformed itself into a young white male homosexual epidemic in Manhattan. In truth, this is not biologically possible. Nevertheless, the leading corporate AIDS experts carefully avoid all discussion of this issue. The U.S. media have censored all serious discussion of AIDS as a manmade disease.

The disease in Africa began in the cities, and not in the jungles. And the most important point of the matter is that the genetic makeup of the AIDS virus does not exist in man or primates. So not only is it improbable that the virus came from monkeys, it's impossible.

There is in fact a mass of circumstantial and scientific evidence that proves absolutely that American gays and black Africans were targeted for genocide via vaccine programs by America's military-medical-industrial complex and agents of the CIA.

A.H. Passarella, a Defense Department official, has recently confirmed HIV is a synthetic biological agent. The evidence is overwhelming, the United States Government and the World Health Organization collaborated on the development, production and proliferation of a synthetic biological agent that subsequently became known as HIV and AIDS.

It is a fact that people are unwittingly used as guinea pigs in covert medical experiments. The Army's LSD experiments, the Tuskegee syphilis experiment, Agent Orange, the exploding Persian Gulf War Syndrome, the human radiation experiments, as well as hundreds of documented bio-warfare experiments were conducted by the military on unsuspecting civilians. And the National Academy of Sciences is silent on its cooperative role with the military in the development of secret biological weapons for mass killing.

Since the middle '70s, some 30 million people worldwide have died from AIDS and another 42 million currently have the disease, according to the BBC. It is also generally known by many that sex has nothing to do with the transmission of the disease.

After AIDS, the most publicized recent vaccination tragedy appears to be what happened to U.S. soldiers who served in the Gulf War, 1990-91. Virtually all the deaths, both of veterans and their families, are linked to two things: exposure to depleted-uranium ammunition, which causes cancer rates to skyrocket, and the vaccinations they received before they left to fight against Iraq.

The agony of American servicemen poisoned by their own government with coerced inoculations has been demonically exquisite. Here are excerpts from a report to a 1994 Senate committee:

> Many Gulf War couples also report that they are no longer able to make love. Intercourse causes the women to experience immediate abdominal cramping and intense burning sensations, as though their genitals were being torched. For many, their labias crack and bleed. Also, the semen burns both husband and wife within minutes of contact with skin. It causes open sores—blisters that bleed.
>
> Many Gulf War families are being advised against pregnancy. Babies are being born with extra toes and fingers, undeveloped lungs, and missing body parts. One child was born with an oversized umbilical cord that wrapped around his body six times, nearly strangling him. This child appears to be developmentally delayed and exhibits other debilitating symptoms similar to his father's. Another child was born without a thyroid gland. She also has dozens of tumors all over her body and inside her mouth. Still another child has intermittent vaginal bleeding.
>
> One Gulf War spouse had two miscarriages in the year after her husband's return. She complains of headaches, rashes, and frequent vaginal infections. In a third pregnancy, a son was delivered two months premature. The child required three months of

> intensive care and numerous painful operations. He now has vision and hearing problems, a lung ailment, and cerebral palsy. This woman has subsequently miscarried again.

Sen. John D. Rockefeller IV, chair of the Committee on Veterans' Affairs United States Senate Hearing, in 1994 summed it all up perfectly:

> The results of our investigation showed a reckless disregard that shocked me, and I think they will shock all Americans. The use of investigational drugs in the Persian Gulf is especially troublesome. The Pentagon . . . threw caution to the winds, ignoring all warnings of potential harm, and gave these drugs to hundreds of thousands of soldiers with virtually no warnings and no safeguards. If that wasn't bad enough, they administered these drugs and vaccines in such a way that there is a very good chance they wouldn't have even worked for the intended purpose. They would not have protected most soldiers from chemical or biological warfare.

This preceding information was taken from "Immunization Theory vs. Reality: Exposé on Vaccinations," Copyright 1996, by Neil Z. Miller.

In 2002 it was discovered Gulf War illness is closely associated with an abnormal immune response to squalene, a substance used to enhance the transmission of medications (http://www.whale.to/v/garry.html).

Dr. Renate Engler, chief of immunology at Walter Reed Army Medical Center addressed a conference on the anthrax vaccine policy at Ft. Detrick, Maryland on 25–27 May 1999. Dr. Engler reported many having chronic systemic reactions to the anthrax vaccine during the fall of 1998 (http://www.whale.to/v/anthrax3.html).

Squalene is a substance detected in both Gulf War vaccines and more recently anthrax vaccines given to service personnel. Squalene is NOT an FDA-approved substance and its consequences on health are unknown. As a vaccine booster ingredient, it is thought to increase immunity, but its use has been denied time and again by the Pentagon. Now they have been caught by scientific studies.

The revelation on squalene more clearly establishes that the Pentagon may be conducting "medical experiments" on service members. Other Congressional hearings have already established that the Pentagon conducted *de facto* experiments because it avoided organization-level FDA review concerning the way the vaccine is used and administered.

While there are numerous other medical horror stories to be told about various untested or inauthentically tested substances that have been foisted on the American people (including Aspartame, the brainchild of one-time Searle Pharmaceutical president Donald Rumsfeld), this article will just touch on one more aspect, one more thing to think about when you realize the U.S. government can make you take shots you can't refuse.

The Possibility of Implants Without Your Permission

Dr. Rod Lewis, in an article reprinted on the Conspiracy Planet website, alleges that drug giants want to sell 3 billion doses of the smallpox vaccine to the feds. He further notes:

> As reported about 6 months ago in *Industry Standard* magazine, Hitachi has developed a microchip, known as the MU chip, that is only .04mm square with 128K of memory and can emit a RF (radio frequency) signal up to two feet. It can be woven into currency or used in biological tissue—It is completely transparent.
>
> Also, don't forget L.U.C.I.D. and our friends at Digital Demon — ahem, I mean Angel. What is Project LUCID? Well, according to conspiracy investigator Texe Marrs:
>
> A frightening behemoth is rising up from the depths of America's hidden SS establishment. Like a vast and monstrous silicon octopus, Project L.U.C.I.D. is stretching forth its ominous and threatening, high tech tentacles. Multitudes of unsuspecting, helpless victims will very soon be encircled and crushed by Big Brother's new, Gestapo police state. Who among us can possibly escape from the electronic cages now being prepared for all mankind?

Dr. Lewis is a bit less hysterical, but no less insistent on offering us a warning, although he does outline a scenario in which the chip is implanted right over your old smallpox scar, if you've had a previous vaccination. The government or one its rogue elements lets smallpox loose in Smalltown, USA—sure they can sacrifice a few thousand more Americans to make the empire more secure. The whole country panics and lines up for their vaccine. They go to predesignated public health service offices and fill out forms with all kinds of ID questions . . .

The information is put into a computer and the computer programs the little MU which is dropped into the vaccine bottle with your name on it. You step up for the pneumatic injection and *voilá*, you are a walking database and transmitter.

Lewis then theorizes in the event of some sort of national emergency, the government will then be able to identify those with chips, based on extensive computer files of each individual, who are friend or foe. If you're a foe, your access to your own money, medical care and food would automatically be terminated—a chilling scenario, to be sure, but one that can't be ruled out given the draconian, fascist tactics that have brought the Homeland Security idea to this point.

Two other vaccine-related stories deserve mention in this essay—the hidden kicker in the Salk polio vaccine that produced cancers 30 years later, and current furor over the alleged link between the MMR vaccine and autism.

Attorneys for the Bush Administration asked a federal court in December 2002 to order that documents on hundreds of cases of autism allegedly caused by childhood vaccines be kept from the public. Department of Justice lawyers asked a special master in the US Court of Federal Claims to seal the documents, arguing that allowing their automatic disclosure would take away the right of federal agencies to decide when and how the material should be released.

Attorneys for the families of hundreds of autistic children charged that the government was trying to keep the information out of civil courts, where juries might be convinced to award large judgments against vaccine manufacturers.

The court is currently hearing approximately 1,000 claims brought by the families of autistic children. The suits charge that the measles-mumps-rubella (MMR) vaccine, which until recently included a mercury-containing preservative known as thimerosal, can cause neurological damage leading to autism.

Now, with all of these examples of horrific government behavior in vaccine programs, the question becomes: How can the vast majority of legislators in the United States vote for a bill (the Homeland Security bill) that allows the government to give these kinds of shots and punish people for refusing them, given all the evidence of past abuse of these programs? What kind of beasts would vote for this without even reading the legislation? The U.S. Congress, that's who. Beasts, far more interested in large cash payments from pharmaceutical giants than the health of the American people.

Dr. Alan Cantwell, author of "AIDS and the Doctors of Death" and many other articles on the disease, says:

> Is the fear of vaccines justified? It is clear that vaccines can be dangerous. The contamination of vaccines is a reality, and vaccine experiments can be hazardous to one's health. AIDS, unknown two decades ago, is now an increasing worldwide epidemic with millions of deaths predicted for the next decade. Could vaccines contaminated with cancer-causing and immunosuppressive viruses unleash new plagues in the New Millennium? If so, the new plagues may be far worse than the diseases we eradicated by vaccine programs in the twentieth century.

The situation that exists is this: if you take the government-ordered shots, there is a high probability you will sicken and die, and the government will wind up with your property; if you refuse the shots, you will be incarcerated in a government-run vaccine-refusers detention camp, where the likelihood is you will be killed anyway, and the government will wind up with your property.

The current Homeland Security measures may be likened to the Catholic Inquisition of medieval times, where accused devil-worshippers were flung into a lake to determine the verdict against them. If they sank and drowned, they were determined to be innocent, and the church got their property. If they floated, they were judged guilty, put to death, and the church got their property.

So the words of George W. Bush are just a new variation of that old fascist scam: you're either with me or against me, and if you're against me, you're dead. This is the way it now is in the country that used to be America.

9

The new resistance

Fingers of frost creep across our December windows as we fire up our computers long before dawn to check the latest atrocity from Washington, the latest affront to the honesty and dignity of the human race. I imagine that I and my circle of Internet friends must be somewhat like the French Resistance of its time, spreading the latest rumors of war and trying to debunk false charges of terror laid at our feet by men who pretend to be our leaders but who are really the stooges of a foreign power, an alien menace even, these soulless men who run the banks, keep us in chains, and obliterate our Constitution in the process.

Perhaps the Resistance analogy is a little overdrawn. I mean, we don't have Nazi stormtroopers bearing down on us with guns drawn . . . . yet. Although there was an incident in Eugene, Oregon a short while ago. . . .

The new Resistance is definitely online, checking out the latest tirade from a new cadre of great writers, great pursuers of liberty, Arundhati Roy in India, Chris Floyd in Moscow, Mike Ruppert in Los Angeles, Al Giordano in Central America and voices from a thousand principled stops in between. The new Resistance is checking out Web radio—Jeff Rense, Alex Jones, Meria Heller and many others—because there you can hear what's actually happening, not what corporate banker radio would like you to believe is going on with fascist phonies like Rush Limbaugh and the prominent Moonie, Pat Robertson.

The new revolution is you and me, and is definitely not being reported in the newspapers, who keep telling us Bush's popularity is at an all-time high and give us not a whisper that the evil men in the White House who are allowed to keep their lucrative secrets by judges who rule against the people's right to know are the very same men who appointed those very same judges, a rancid closed circle of horror that lets the guilty rich go free and jails poor innocents without trial, without phone call, without hope.

Each day a new horror, stories eagerly passed around from computer to computer, from state to state and country to country. Just when we thought it would be hard to top the Wellstone incident for sheer horror—oh, the FAA can't figure out what happened; well, WE all instantly figured out what happened!—along comes the Kissinger debacle. Henry Kissinger to ferret out what really happened on 9/11. Well, if my name isn't Ho Chi Minh!

And just when we think Kissinger can't be topped as an outrage to freedom and justice, the lead story in my Sunday paper yesterday was Bush declaring he can kill whomever he wants to merely on his own say so.

This is what America has come to—making lists of people who can be killed on the spot.

First Bush passed a law saying he could keep people in jail without trial and without lawyer and without phone call merely on the say so of any of his totally corrupt functionaries. Now he's graduated to saying he can kill anyone he pleases merely on whim—sure, sure, they'll produce "evidence," but as in the case with Iraq and this funny group named al-Qaeda (the one that nobody ever seems to be able to find until some Nazi [read: U.S. or Israel] government arrests them and releases a neatly packaged photo and bio), they don't ever have to release the "evidence." They just have to say they have it, and then Tony Blair will get up and freak out about how dangerous these folks are, the ones that they have the "evidence" against, kind of like what happened right after 9/11, when Blair insisted we had this irrefutable "evidence" against Osama bin Laden, which we still have not, by the way, seen.

And as long as I'm going in this direction, let me point something out: The real purpose of 9/11, it seems to me, was to demonize

Muslims, to make public consciousness more amenable to going to war against Muslim countries. Most people have accepted the general drift of media coverage and accepted bin Laden's guilt, accepted that this was a Muslim conspiracy, Muslims who drank and went to strip clubs and used cocaine, devout Muslims who gave their lives for the holy terror against the West "because they envied our freedom."

Have you ever heard anything stupider than that assertion? Well, yes, actually—that anybody believes that story!

We must not completely forget that Osama bin Laden may not actually exist—except in the minds of war publicists. It is already a virtual certainty that this dreaded al-Qaeda bunch is actually a department of the U.S. CIA, designed to wreak fake terror in order to facilitate more oppressive laws to keep the unruly population in check.

When you start to track this whole terror suicide tangent, you run across something else that you may not have noticed and that you certainly won't read in big newspapers, especially the biggest newspaper, the *New York Times*. It's that long-ago Lyndon LaRouche assertion that Hamas and Islamic Jihad have received funding from Israel because they oppose the PLO; yes, that's Israel funding terror against itself. Why would they do that? Think about it. Why were those Israelis cheering in New Jersey right after the towers were hit? Think about who benefits from terror. Think about why 9/11 really happened and why you don't read a single thing about this in the newspapers, even though it is the most important subject to be thinking about in all the world.

Well, you can bet my friends and I in the new resistance are thinking about it, every day and at all times. Let's face it: Nazi bankers have taken over the world and are trying to turn every country into a combination of plantations run by them and concentration camps containing us. George W. Bush wants every country in the world to be exactly like Honduras, where the killer villains are in charge, ordinary people have no say, and rich criminals far away steal the bulk of that country's value and the local populace is drugged or bludgeoned into silence. That is, as they say, the Republican message of today.

America is making war on its own people, and using convicted and as yet uncaught criminals to do it: felon John Poindexter tracking the secret facts of Americans. Now that is simply Hitlerian. John Ashcroft is a felon who simply has not yet been arrested.

And George W. Bush? You want the list? (Note the number of death penalty offenses he has committed!) How about starting with military desertion in time of war? Of course, there is the cocaine smuggling, although they say Jeb deserves most of the credit for that. And then there would be the blatant looting of banks during the S&L fire sales in the 1980s, although his father deserves most of the credit for that.

The most frequent criminal activity of George W. Bush, of course, would be obstruction of justice, given the people he has hired and the laws he has abrogated to further the criminal activities of his father and his friends. Are you listening, Kenny Boy? And of course, the crime we're really trying to pin on him, other than treason for his willful destruction of the Constitution, would be mass murder, both for presiding over the inside job on 9/11 and for the needless invasion of Afghanistan, just to make his pipeline plan and drug smuggling work.

New charges will doubtless be available after he starts using up more military ordnance on Iraq. And who knows? The sky's the limit for this guy, truly the most evil American president ever.

And worse, it's not only the president who—if the world were a just and honest place—should be indicted for mass murder and treason, but a MAJORITY of the U.S. Congress, too, who has voted for his totalitarian initiatives . . . . let's just say anybody who took a contribution from Enron should now be in jail.

And right now the United States is making war, right in front of our noses, in more than a dozen countries, and on the wrong side of honor and justice—against the rights of the people—in every single case.

Land of the free and the home of the brave? Shit! Land of the duped and home of the chickenshit chickenhawks!

The big one is not really Afghanistan or Iraq—it's Colombia, where rapidly increasing numbers of U.S. troops are preparing for action next door in Venezuela, but also in Ecuador, Peru and Brazil, all countries in which people-power movements have broken out.

The United States, of course, has always been at war in Central America, maintaining murderous dictatorships in Guatemala, Honduras, Nicaragua and El Salvador, where ordinary people have no chance of living decent lives. And of course you know about the continuing activities in Indonesia and the Philippines (the latter a country in which we have conducted covert operations for more than 100 years, by the way).

The farcical situation continues in the Middle East, where Nazi Eretz Israel continues its obliteration of Palestinian babies and old women—the U.S. newspapers reverse the nomenclature because they are owned by either Jews or Zionists: it's really Jewish terrorists and Palestinian freedom fighters, not the other way around, and has been so since 1948 (if not before), when the Jews first started killing the natives, stealing their land, and then changing the names of the villages, hoping no one would notice what they were doing.

And Iraq. What a horrible joke. There was no legitimate reason for the first Gulf War and there is even less justification for this one, except that Bush wants to steal their oil and the sleeping American populace, further anesthetized by the CNN/Fox daily parade of lies called "Showdown with Iraq," seems reluctant to stand in the way of this latest chapter of Christian crusade against the heathens.

That there is no evidence against Iraq is clearly reflected in Bush's attempt to come up with some new trumped up charge at least once a week. War by propaganda. America does not now nor has it ever cared who it kills, and that is the one big horror that Americans refuse to face: why the Bush cabal, and the Clinton cabal before it, get away with what they do, which is killing innocent people for profit. That's what America has always done, since the days of killing 60 million Indians.

That's what America does: it kills innocent people for money.

So . . . . you won't read that in most newspapers but I do hear it talked about frequently on the web, among my friends, George in Switzerland, Jeanne in Poland, Steen in Denmark, Big Bob in Sweden, Jack Riddler in Berlin, Tim in Ireland, Jared at the Hague, Rick in Azerbaijan, Zsolt in Budapest, Al in North Dakota, Rick in

Arkansas, Mary in Tallahassee, Helen and Judith in New Hampshire, Dick in Yakima, Ken in Phoenix, David in Portland, Will in Vancouver, Alistair in New Zealand . . . I know of hundreds and they all know of thousands and probably they all know of millions who are constantly talking about that what you read in the big newspapers are lies—that our freedom is being stolen by bankers, arms makers and politicians who would just as soon murder their own children (ritually murder, for you Bohemian Grove fans out there) as let an opportunity slip by to make a buck.

The group I know on the Internet realizes that the U.S. government sends troops to Colombia ostensibly to fight the war on drugs, but the real purpose of this effort is to ASSURE THE FLOW of drugs, not to eradicate the crop, because the feds are simply making way too much money on this crop to ever want to destroy it. The deals in Kosovo, Macedonia, the Stans and to some extent Iraq are also about this. My group knows this. The big newspapers write little about it. The group I talk with every day realizes pretty much as a group that the last U.S. election was totally fixed—that democracy is dead in the United States—because of the electronic voting machines that can be manipulated both before and after the fact—and also I think during. This means that anyone who was declared the winner in any given election last month (are you listening, Norm Coleman?) did not necessarily win that election, but there is no way to check.

This goes hand-in-hand with the Patriot Act and Homeland Security Department—totally fake democracy all around. That the media and Congress approve of these measures simply means these are people who should not be listened to, never mind voted for.

People talking on the web know you shouldn't ever take a government immunization and that the real reason for them is to make lots of money for some pharmaceutical giant. We also realize there probably is no new big medical problem today that was not developed in some black budget government lab.

So each morning, we rise before dawn, turn on our computers, and see what stories our friends and the new day will bring. Later that night, we in the new resistance still toil in front of our screens, bleary-eyed, to squeeze out one more message to our friends about some organized peace activities or consumer medical alert or to beware of some new scam invented by some government PR criminal. If you have any feelings about the need for freedom and the ability to say whatever you want, we'd like you to join the new resistance. But you're going to have to have a computer.

It is the way of the real world now. The real people are on the Internet, trying to let others know about the lethal lies that are being foisted upon us at every turn. The fake people are sending press releases to totally cynical and unreliable newspapers, urging others to support the War on Terror, without really realizing (or worse, perhaps they do!) that the war on terror is really a war on freedom, perhaps their very own.

10

Guilty until proven innocent: The new American way

Guilty until proven innocent. This is the new American way. And no evidence is necessary to order someone killed. Just the say-so of the man with the gun.

Everything Americans have worked for over the past 227 years, to establish the rule of law over the emotions of the mob and the predations of the aristocracy, has been nullified by fake terror, insincere legislators and endless bribery.

Vigilante justice is the new order of the day in this frightening 2003 edition of the United States of America. Due process, the right to a fair trial, the right to be safe and secure in one's home—these are all things of the past, things we used to defend as the best traits of American freedom in those happy days before the self-inflicted War on Terror (*see note at the end of the chapter).

Now we are defending the right of the president to order people killed because he says they are bad guys. He doesn't need any evidence because he's the president, according to Ari Fleischer, his sycophantic press secretary. This is what we are presenting to our children as the actions of a democracy.

As the reptilian politician Henry Hyde said recently, the Constitution is just not relevant anymore. What he means is people don't have rights anymore. What seems to be the surest guarantee toward success in America these days is a criminal conviction incurred while participating in the wholesale fleecing of the American population. As in the cases of John Poindexter, Eliot Abrams and Ollie North (both George Bushes could also be in this category were the judiciary more honest), guilty verdicts in service to the hidden hand of the power elite are a sure way to find full employment in this era of runaway corruption.

Guilty until proven innocent. Look at poor pathetic Saddam. Nothing he says counts, ever since he had that conversation with U.S. ambassador April Glaspie, who told him the U.S. wouldn't really mind if he invaded Kuwait. So because he had a legitimate grievance—slant drilling/theft of oil by the Sabah family—he did invade. And what a penalty! A half million Iraqis dead (mostly children) and 13 years later, the U.S. is still bombing him. What did he do against the United States? Nothing. He was our ally. But we set him up. All other U.S. "allies" should be taking note of this behavior, but I doubt that they are. Just like in our country, the leaders of those countries who took large amounts of money to be our allies are too busy concealing their blood money to be genuinely interested in the fate of their own people. Just ask Hosni Mubarak, or Prince Whatshisname? That Saudi sultan who mostly hangs out in Monte Carlo and insists he's a devout Muslim. Just like the supposed hijackers were devout Muslims. And speaking of the hijackers, they are definitely guilty until proven innocent. I heard it on CNN, and also from Tony Blair.

And even if we didn't get their names right, they're still guilty until proven innocent, no matter who they are or what names they use.

It's "them" and they're guilty. Just ask your president.

Guilty until proven innocent. Osama bin Laden. Does he really exist? Are any of his tapes legit? And if he does exist, isn't he a CIA operative? He used to be, when he first started getting financial assistance from Washington. This is why the feds blocked John O'Neill's investigation. He was about to find out that bin Laden was working for the CIA, and that those embassy hits in Africa were done by the Mossad, not by Islamic Jihad (although there is some debate about the actual difference between the two). But we had solid evidence against bin Laden, Blair said so. He just wouldn't tell us what it was. And that's why 5,000 Afghanis had to die, even though there never really was any intention to catch bin Laden (if he really exists). But those Afghanis were guilty because they couldn't prove their innocence—they couldn't prove they didn't facilitate the destruction of two skyscrapers in New York—and that's why they had to die, in a hail of anonymous bunker busters from 30,000 feet.

Guilty until proven innocent. Timothy McVeigh! Remember him. He supposedly parked a truck bomb in front of a big building. This bomb supposedly blew down this big building, killed a lot of mothers and babies, but amazingly failed to knock down a sapling right next to the truck. The Air Force general who said that building came down as a result of many major explosives attached to stanchions inside the building was never listened to. An Oklahoma City cop who was gathering information mysteriously committed suicide. A federal agent who had all sorts of testimony about Iraqis in the neighborhood was told to shut up and drummed out of the BATF.

And McVeigh—remember him? He was guilty until proven innocent. One of the witnesses at his execution said he never did stop breathing. A story much later in the *Weekly World News* (that paragon of journalistic integrity—whoops! "Statue of Elvis Found on Mars!)—insisted that McVeigh never was executed, had had plastic surgery, took steroids, and was living on an island in the state of Idaho. Well, wouldn't you know the building where that story and that newspaper were published was the first place hit in the anthrax attacks. Poor Bob Stevens, the fellow who died in that attack. He was clearly guilty until proven innocent.

Guilty until proven innocent. Paul Wellstone, liberal Minnesota senator "accidentally" killed in a plane crash shortly before an election.

Guilty until proven innocent. Mel Carnahan, liberal Missouri senator "accidentally" killed in a plane crash shortly before an election.

Guilty until proven innocent. Vicki Weaver. A bullet in the head for being married to a man who was set up by the feds. That man who shot her, FBI sniper Lon Horiuchi, was clearly guilty but ruled innocent by a federal judge (after the feds gave Randy Weaver several million in hopes he'd keep his mouth shut, which he didn't).

Guilty until proven innocent. Those 25 dead children at David Koresh's burned out compound in Waco, whom a Fox reporter called collateral damage. Those kids will never be proven innocent. They were guilty and deserved to be slaughtered by the U.S. government, according to federal agents who participated in the raid, who helped in the killing of children and then denied they did.

Guilty until proven innocent. The Egyptian dupes who participated in the first attack on the World Trade Center, who were guided by an FBI informant who tried to get his controllers to stop the attack, but the FBI guys in charge preferred instead to let the bomb go off.

Who is guilty? Who is innocent? It's almost as if whoever Bush says is guilty is actually innocent and vice versa. I mean, Cheney is clearly guilty of obstruction of justice in the California energy crisis because his closest colleagues made millions of dollars and the vice president refuses to divulge any of the details of his energy meetings. Why? They were planning how to rip off California. It's so obvious. Poindexter was guilty of lying about the Reagan-Bush October Surprise and now is in charge of watching all of us.

The same logic can be applied to the latest World Trade Center cover-up. The Patriot Act and Homeland Security Department were invented not to protect U.S. security from terrorist infiltration; they were devised to keep people from discovering the true culprits of the 9/11 attacks, and you can be sure many of them live in and around Washington.

So let's switch things around: let's give these power elite pigs a dose of their own medicine. Let's play by the very rules that they have created for us—their minions, their budsters (columnist Al Martin quoting Dubya: BUDsters stands for broke, useless and depressed).

Their logic is that people they suspect of uncovering any evidence that implicates the Bush cartel in anything are automatically "enemy combatants," "against us instead of with us," and liable to be imprisoned incommunicado without the previously usual

Constitutional protection and right to a fair trial. (How could anybody get a fair trial now anyway with all the judges these clowns have appointed, all these insincere political functionaries rather than jurists with actual integrity?)

As with Saddam and bin Laden, and a host of other U.S. puppet dictators we have used over time and then discarded when they got too big for their britches, the U.S. media machine can say anything at all about these fools and get away with it, without a whit of proof.

Rumsfeld keeps letting the real deal slip: the U.S. keeps planting phony stories in media around the world, and then says, no, we're not planting phony stories.

They can say anything they want, without a shred of evidence, and get away with it, because the big boys own all the big media and the vast majority of the little people are just too timid, too powerless, to confront the status quo.

Well, if they can say anything they want, then we can too.

Guilty until proven innocent: George W. Bush, Dick Cheney and the Carlyle Group gang, Baker, Carlucci, Colin Powell and Poppy Bush. Under the laws they have devised for the American people, they are now guilty until proven innocent of mass murder and treason, incomprehensibly grand theft, too many counts of obstruction of justice to even enumerate, and perhaps the worst crime of all, the destruction of the American Constitution, the very document, the principles that make America America.

What are we fighting for if we don't have that? Their right to unbridled corporate greed? To hell with that. I'm not fighting for that. If you, by your silence, choose to fight for that, you are surely guilty until proven innocent.

I believe it is time to start judging these people who are making all these Nazi-type laws by these laws themselves. Bush and Cheney need to be in jail indefinitely, without access to counsel or family, for multiple counts of obstruction of justice, for widespread theft in the Enron, Harken, and Halliburton examples, where they have crafted laws (the vaccine orders and the invasion of Afghanistan) to directly benefit friends and members of their own families through government contracts.

The younger Bush is directly involved in a conflict of interest when his father owns portions of several of the companies which have directly benefited from his recent decisions.

The real terrorists are Bush, Cheney and the big business cabal. Right now they are terrorizing the American people and all the people in the world by creating cynical unjust laws and then enforcing them with crooked cops and crooked judges.

With all the lies they have told about their business dealings, and all the false accusations they have made about Saddam and his supposed weapons of mass destruction (that America itself sold to him; Rumsfeld himself brokered the deal), we have every reason—EVERY REASON, WITH GOD AS OUR WITNESS—to believe they are lying about what happened at the World Trade Center. It was the worst crime in American history, and they committed it. And now they are committing even more crimes against every decent, law-abiding person in the world.

They are clearly guilty, and I doubt very much they can prove their innocence. It is now time for every person in the world to insist that they try before the court of public opinion, and before God.

Let all the lying—and the cringing in fear—stop now.

Let's have the truth—now.

Without a shadow of a doubt, they are all guilty until proven innocent.

And I personally don't think they can "prove" their innocence without a massive police presence.

* The phrase was "self-inflicted War on Terror." The War on Terror is self-inflicted either way you slice it: if the American power elite was behind the 9/11 attacks, well, it's obviously self-inflicted; if it's really true that foreign terrorists actually devised the 9/11 attacks, they did it in response to the American oppression of Third World countries, and in particular by supporting dreadful tyrannies in their respective homelands. Either way, the War on Terror is self-inflicted by Americans upon Americans, and uses agents of different nationalities to carry out certain supporting aspects of the terror.

11

A curtain of sleep

An examination of the Generation Gap in the 21st Century reveals a morbid twist of fate

Hello? Are you there? (Can't tell.) Am I getting through?

I need to give you a warning. Can you understand?

The information you needed did not get through. From the time just after you went to school as a kid . . . to about five minutes ago . . . the information you have received has been mostly lies.

All the people I talk to . . . who can understand what I'm saying . . . they're all about sixty years old. (Hello!) Much younger than that can't understand. The information you needed to thrive and prosper did not get through.

I think it's the schools. Everyone should get out of the schools. Don't believe what they're saying. You've been taught to take bribes and keep your mouth shut. Don't do it.

It used to be just the opposite. When I was twenty, the old people—of whom I guess I am one now—didn't have a clue. Maybe it was the Beatles? Or marijuana? Or the CIA LSD experiments? Or all three.

Now, it seems the only people who notice what's going on are old and decrepit like me. Oh sure, there are indymedia protests and such, but most kids don't pay attention to their freedom evaporating in a landslide of phony patriotism, corporate hogwash raining down on us like pronouncements from God to Moses on the mountain. I guess that's true of all the generations, though. Most don't pay attention.

I've noticed in my transit through this life that music seems to imbed itself in your brain most in your late twenties. Something about fluidity of the inner ear creating a free-flowing balance that allows sound, particularly music, to work its wonderful way down into your synapses. So all your life you're stuck with whatever you listened to then. I'm lucky. I got the "Marrakech Express." And Gil Scott-Heron's "Johannesburg." Some people got the BeeGees, poor souls. But after that—almost everything after that, from David Bowie on—is corporate rock.

Approved by the suits in the boardroom. Very little human about it. Strictly a business deal. Not really healthy stuff.

The point being: Back when the music was good, it seemed that public issues were more widely understood. Nixon didn't get away with his crap. Today he would. Bush is getting away with his crap. I blame it on the music, on corporate control of creative options, mostly manifested through the rigidity of schools, that focus on creating lackey stooges rather than individuals with integrity. In fact, you probably never heard that in your passage through schools: individuals with integrity.

The information you needed did not get through. It was diverted for the profits of a few. The misery of the millions was substituted. Teachers became businessmen. The contentment of civilization was diverted for the profits of a few.

How can you identify the point at which it happened? You can track it from the point in the late '60s or early '70s when the percentage of hourly pay began to not rise in relation to the Gross National Product, or maybe that point in the late '50s when women started going to work (I'm not saying that's bad, but I am saying it changed the financial picture, and made big bucks for the power elite).

Wages have been essentially frozen since 1972. Sure, the numbers reflected by inflation have risen, but prices have risen much more drastically than wages. All that money has been stolen by the power elite, and all this time the big newspapers (which are owned by the power elite) have been saying everything was OK. The politicians, too.

The information you needed did not get through.

I don't think I'm just acting old, here. I think I am describing a phenomenon that actually happened, and I feel the need to try to warn you—you folks younger than myself—that everything you have been taught has been twisted for the purpose of profit. And if you say that, well, profit is the purpose of life, then that will be a sure sign that you have in fact been twisted.

The Land of the Free and the Home of the Brave is really a vicious corporate entity that has been making war on the rest of the world for the entire 20th century . . . oh, not the people, of course. People are decent everywhere, if they have enough to eat. No, not the people, the movers and shakers. From the rape of the Philippines in 1899 to the target practice in Iraq in 2002, America has been at war with everyone, but has managed to convince its own populace that it was fighting for freedom. Yeah, the freedom to rip off everybody else in the world.

Did you ever notice all America's best allies—like Saudi Arabia, Pakistan, Egypt, Colombia—are vicious dictatorships? Didn't that ever puzzle you? Doesn't it bother you when America has to bribe other countries to get them to agree?

The information you needed did not get through.

Did you realize Bush's grandfather was once busted for sending money to Hitler? Check it out. You might see how the Nazi line survived all these years—no, not Hitler himself, but the vicious, deceptive, racist philosophy—is now in full bloom in Washington. If you don't see that—and say something about it very soon and very loud—the price you are going to pay is going to be much higher than you thought. In fact, you may not be able to pay such a high price in your entire lifetime.

Did you realize that all this talk about God that you hear from so many people is really just Freud's concept of transference? Most of us grow up in the safety of our parents' house and from the time we are little kids have an authority figure to protect us from danger; then when we grow up, we fail to leave that childhood mode and adopt some imaginary parent in the sky that enables us to continue, childlike, throughout our lives. It is this kind of behavior that makes us so vulnerable to the lethal lies of politicians and priests who say they are going to lead us toward freedom and prosperity, not to mention eternal bliss. And then they molest us.

Wake up! The information you needed did not get through.

Now we all find ourselves in a situation where the country has been turned into a killer police state by a cynical band of petronazis—really, the 235 families who have ruled the world since the time of Charlemagne—who have plans to herd us all into camps, all those people who do not have a salary of $100,000 per year or more, and who can contribute much of it in the form of bribes to the power elite. The powers that be have decided there are too many people in the world and the world's population needs to be reduced by THREE QUARTERS in order for them to live comfortable, pollution-free lives.

So there you have the reason for what's going on: war in almost every nation on earth. Cuts down the population nicely. Especially kids. It's good to kill kids in a war because that obliterates future generations, which is what they try to do when trying to reduce populations. They're doing a lot of that in Israel nowadays.

Diseases in medicines. Very effective at killing large numbers, as has been demonstrated by the successes with smallpox vaccines containing HIV in both Africa and the gay communities in New York and San Francisco.

Psychotronic devices. Maximize diseases in people, makes them take more medicines (good for Eli Lilly profits) and makes them die sooner (saves space).

Poison the food supply. Maybe this started with fluoride, a nuke waste by-product they had to find a use for. Now we have aspartame, invented and purveyed by one Donald Rumsfeld. They say if used long enough it will give you the same symptoms as heart trouble, or, come to think of it, psychotronic devices.

And have you heard about the list of designer diseases? Some say West Nile virus is the latest success. But there's Mad Cow, Ebola, hanta . . . hey, when it comes to eliminating lives, they spare no expense.

The information you needed did not get through.

You have access to more information than any other generation on Earth, yet you are the most poorly educated generation in history.

Past a certain point in time . . . I'm not sure when it was . . . but it has something to do with TV: if you grew up with TV, chances are excellent you're not a real human being, you're a TV character and your life is some sick sitcom in which you are totally powerless . . . and clueless.

Past a certain point in time . . . you can see the progression in the degeneration of American literature throughout the 20th century . . . past that point and you didn't get the information to make you self-reliant, you didn't get Emerson, you didn't get a respect for your neighbors and a disbelief in politicians. Most of all . . . perhaps . . . you didn't get all those good old journalists who told you to check both sides of the story. None of those journalists are left now.

Otherwise, the information you needed would have gotten through.

The people who are aware of the civilization-busting measures now taking place, at least the ones I see, are all very old and gray.

The kids aren't here. Because of this the future is a lot bleaker than it ought to be.

The information they needed did not get through.

12

Ghost dance

Winter solstice of a species
December 21, 2002

Tomorrow's leftover lies layering the scars in your eyes.
—John Trudell, "Bad Dog"

One hundred twelve years later, the human species sits frightened, wrapped in its security blankets, hunched by its hearthfires, awaiting the same inexorable, unstoppable technological doom that erased Sitting Bull and his Sioux family from the face of the Earth on the snowy plains of South Dakota in the year of our Lord 1890.

It was the Ghost Dance that had made the white man nervous, they said. A five-day paroxysm of ritual that united the living with their deceased ancestors was what totally freaked out the Bible-thumping whites, who, like Christopher Columbus, could not understand why these savages refused to accept the Almighty Power of Jesus Christ. In this acceptance, it must be remembered, the natives were required to give up the lush lands they had gently tended for generations, and were expected to move to areas that were of no use to anyone else. This was the will of God, and the American government. As a result, just like Columbus, just like the Israelites in the Old Testament, the jittery American heroes felt justified and holy when they slaughtered the hapless pagans.

Who knows what small events make fights start, make wars break out? Just as the white man broke every single treaty he ever made with the original inhabitants of the Western Hemisphere (103, I think it was; we kept none; we're still breaking them, here and elsewhere), it was a stray shot that rang out and the shooting started. Or so the white man's history recounts.

Killed was the last great American Indian leader, Sitting Bull, and the faded remnants of once a great nation of hunter/gatherers, who exhibited a respect for nature and the land that has not really been seen since. This paltry, starving group took its place among the nameless corpses of 60 million human beings eradicated from the sacred Earth in the drive by "the greatest country the world has ever known," the United States of America, on the way to fulfilling its date with manifest destiny. A manifest destiny of mass murder, repeated over and over, forever and ever, Amen.

As we see in the continued unjust imprisonment of Leonard Peltier and the imminent plans to obliterate Iraq for very spurious reasons, this destiny continues today, with ever renewable fury.

The ghost dance, which after the massacre at Wounded Knee soon faded from widespread Indian practice—but not consciousness—accurately foreshadowed what was to come for the luckless Lakota. Surely, some of innocent souls must have known they were dancing with their own ghosts. We all must surely realize that now, at this very moment, we too are dancing with our own ghosts.

The history of the human race, particularly as it manifests now with all manner of horrific atomic and biological devices poised and aimed to strike more hapless peasant humans with darkly tinted skin, can now be seen as a ghost dance of its own kind, an innate human drive to kill for abstract concepts like "glory" and "freedom" and, God help us, "homeland security." It is a ghost dance, macabre and horrible, all its own. Perhaps this is the single most obvious distinguishing characteristic of the human race.

Though of course it was preceded by millennia of random slaughter from the Stone Age onward, the 19th century extermination of the American Indians became the paradigm of modern imperialist behavior, as the Brahmins of every country find ever more warped reasons to extinguish the lives of the dark-skinned indigenous peoples of the world. In every conflict in every nation—Israel, Iraq, India and throughout Asia and the Americas—it is the colonialist whites who continue to exploit their dark cousins.

The prized commodity may change as time passes—most recently from tea to oil—but the colors of the conquerors and their dead victims do not. The rationales today are cloaked in cryptic economic invective, but at bottom, it is the race issue that divides the planet into haves and have-nots. Every single person of color knows this in their hearts.

Realizing this, racism, then, can be seen as the driving force behind this colonialism and imperialism that threatens, even now, every one of us inhabiting the Earth, for the killer is no less damned than the victim in the hateful system he is forced to live in.

The rise of capitalism in the 16th century in the form of British banks coincides exactly with the rise of African slavery and this horrid legacy continues to be the dark side of American freedom to this very ugly day. If there were no slaves, capitalism would fail, and there you have the evil engine that powers "the greatest nation in human history" and also continues to keep the world in a state of endless war.

So now we can see clearly that the World Trade Organization, or the deceitful brutality perpetrated by the out-of-control Israelis, is nothing more than a continuation of the murderous Crusades that white European rationalists have perpetrated on dark Asian, Arab and African victims since the days of the Roman empire. For all the sophisticated rhetoric, the Crusades have never ended, and now, with weapons of incomprehensibly devastating power about to be unleashed, everyone is threatened by it, both the user and the used.

What is going on now has always been going on, with the vast majority of people far from the battle zones comfortably distracted by their precious material possessions and meaningless quests for social style—not realizing that as accessories to mass murder, they will be just as profoundly affected by this unsolved human riddle as any child disfigured by the evil legacy of depleted uranium ammunition contaminating the earth in the fields where they play.

This is the legacy of civilized human behavior. For all of us, this is our very own ghost dance.

In this time of fear and fascism, however, some people are still trying to think clearly.

The Gaian philosopher William Irwin Thompson writes, if Bush decides to use nuclear weapons against Iraq, we are clearly on the brink of a new dark age and all bets are off for the survival of everyone.

"We ceased being an educated society when television made politics an extension of the entertainment industry," Thompson writes in *Annals of Earth*, Vol. 20, November 2002, in an essay titled "We Become What We Hate."

He notes: "Violence on the part of the state is called military operations; violence of the part of the revolutionaries or the stateless is called terrorism by those holding the monopoly on state violence," and concludes: "One cannot simply put one's faith into one single institution: political, financial, religious, or academic, and trust that its leaders will be right.

"The world knows that there is an Islam that is not that of the terrorists, but does the world know there is an America other than Hollywood, McDonald's and Coca Cola ads that camouflage a foreign policy of arms sales and military support of authoritarian regimes?"

To which I would add, is there . . . really?

Thompson believes we are on the hinge of changing eras, from one of nation states to idea groups.

The founder of the New Age think tank Lindisfarne Foundation, Thompson foresees the world political system in the midst of change from nation-states to philosophical entities and developing systems that are not contained in any one country or any single religion. He also notes that recent democratic progress in Iran, one of the world's oldest continuous nations, and China, which has recently opened itself up to democratic economic reforms, are positive signs on the world's political spectrum, and ones that need to be acknowledged, rather than resisted and exploited by America and her supercilious allies.

But if America continues to try to plunder the rest of the world with its military superiority and financial manipulation, as it appears ready and willing to do, then we are facing a new dark age that will affect everyone in the worst possible way.

Will we wake up, or goosestep our way into oblivion, performing our own ghost dance, like Sitting Bull and his family, for the last time?

The United States broke every treaty it ever made with the indigenous native Americans. This is a telling fact all the peoples of the world should take notice of.

Would that our leaders perform that ghost dance and hear the long-dead echoes of the Arapahoe chant:

Light is Returning
Even though this is the darkest hour
No one can hold
Back the Dawn

• • •

In January 1889, a Paiute Indian, Wavoka, or Jack Wilson, had a revelation during a total eclipse of the sun. It was the genesis of a religious movement that would become known as the Ghost Dance. It was this dance that the Indians believed would reunite them with friends and relatives in the ghost world. As the movement spread from tribe to tribe, it soon took on proportions beyond its original intent and desperate Indians began dancing and singing the songs that would cause the world to open up and swallow all other people while the Indians and their friends would remain on this land, which would return to its beautiful and natural state.

The unity and fervor of the Ghost Dance Movement, however inspired, spurred only fear and hysteria among white settlers, which ultimately contributed to the events ending in the massacre at Wounded Knee.

In the Ghost Dance, Grandfather [a universal title of reverence among Indians and here meaning the messiah] says, when your friends die you must not cry. You must not hurt anybody or do harm to anyone. You must not fight. Do right always. It will give you satisfaction in life. (For more on the Massacre at Wounded Knee in 1890, see http://www.ibiscom.com/knee.htm.)

13

How our schools create sheeple

Why most Americans are unable to perceive and protest America's slide into fascism

> In 1896 the famous John Dewey, then at the University of Chicago, said that independent, self-reliant people were a counter-productive anachronism in the collective society of the future. In modern society, said Dewey, people would be defined by their associations—not by their own individual accomplishments. In such a world people who read too well or too early are dangerous because they become privately empowered, they know too much, and know how to find out what they don't know by themselves, without consulting experts.
>
> —Kurt Johmann, synopsizing John Taylor Gatto

The question on the minds of many people with consciences who are so aghast at the sudden savagery of the new terror-based policies of the U.S. government is: how has the American public so silently and willingly acquiesced to the dishonest and murderous attitudes of George W. Bush and his criminal oil cartel?

The hypnotic power of television is of course one main component of the fearful powerlessness that now grips the American populace and has the rest of the world cringing in fear about where the power elite's military monster will strike next. That is a subject for another time.

The real credit for this continuing American coma belongs to something that has been right in front of our eyes all the time. It's something we have supported, spent our money on and prayed for; something we have participated in ourselves.

The reason Bush has been able to get away with lie after lie in his drive to obliterate our Constitution and install himself as dictator of the world is our public school system. What they did to all of us is directly related to what is happening now in the world.

This connection becomes perfectly obvious when you read Kurt Johmann's essay, "Unschooling: Self-Directed Learning is Best," on his website (http://www.johmann.net/).

Johmann, a software developer who lives in Florida, quotes John Taylor Gatto, an award-winning teacher who taught in New York City government schools for 26 years and quit teaching in 1991 "so he wouldn't harm any more children." Gatto, author of *Dumbing Us Down: The Hidden Curriculum of Compulsory Schooling* and other books investigating the fallacies of public education, insists American public schools teach a hidden curriculum of seven lessons:

1. Confusion. Gatto notes several things contributing to what he calls the lesson of confusion, including: a lack of subject-related context for what is taught; too many unrelated facts and unrelated subjects; a lack of meaning and critical thinking about what is taught.

About this lack of critical thinking Gatto says: "Few teachers would dare to teach the tools whereby dogmas of a school or a teacher could be criticized, since everything must be accepted."

With this kind of training, how would it be possible for a kid to know what valuable things are NOT in public school curricula?

And by extension, how would it be possible for that same adult to discern that what her leaders tell her about American history bears little resemblance to what happened to the victims of those who wrote the histories?

2. Class position. Gatto points to the way students are kept in the same class by age, and, within this age classification, further classified and separated depending on how the students have done schoolwise (for example, classification into so-called gifted classes).

About this lesson Gatto says: "That's the real lesson of any rigged competition like school. You come to know your place."

As someone who has suffered from this myself, you have to ask how many learning opportunities are lost by using rigidly mechanistic criteria that sabotage the process of categorizing children in a productive way.

3. Indifference. For this lesson Gatto is referring to the effects of the ringing bell that announces the end of the current class and the need for students to drop whatever they are doing and proceed to the next class where a different teacher and subject await them.

About bells Gatto says: "Indeed, the lesson of bells is that no work is worth finishing, so why care too deeply about anything?"

And as far as educational evolution goes in kids, this rigidity causes children to assign equal value to all classes, say math and gym, without regard to their relative importance.

4. Emotional dependency. This lesson results from students having to submit to the designated authority, the teacher, regarding their personal desires during class time. As Gatto says: "By stars and red checks, smiles and frowns, prizes, honors, and disgraces, I teach kids to surrender their will to the predestined chain of command."

By the time this learned tendency reaches adulthood, it prevents many people from realizing there may be more qualified candidates other than the two corporate-approved rivals for any given office.

5. Intellectual dependency. This lesson is similar to the lesson of emotional dependency, since both lessons teach students submission to the designated authority. In the case of the lesson of intellectual dependency, the students specifically learn submission to establishment authorities, including the teacher, on intellectual matters.

This definitely discourages thinking "outside the box" when alternatives are presented to any given problem.

As Gatto says: "Successful children do the thinking I assign them with a minimum of resistance and a decent show of enthusiasm. Of the millions of things of value to study, I decide what few we have time for, or actually it is decided by my faceless employers.

". . . Bad kids fight this, of course, even though they lack the concepts to know what they are fighting, struggling to make decisions for themselves about what they will learn and when they will learn it. How can we allow that and survive as schoolteachers? Fortunately [Gatto is being ironic] there are tested procedures to break the will of those who resist . . ."

6. Provisional self-esteem. As Gatto says: "The lesson of report cards, grades, and tests is that children should not trust themselves or their parents but should instead rely on the evaluation of certified officials. People need to be told what they are worth."

As a result, when people get older, they may not be able to determine the worth of a given activity without someone whose authority they covet approving their decision. Put more simply, they may not be able to think for themselves.

7. One cannot hide. By this lesson Gatto means the effect that constant surveillance has on students as they are watched by teachers and other school employees. About the underlying reason for this surveillance Gatto says: ". . . children must be closely watched if you want to keep a society under tight central control. Children will follow a private drummer if you can't get them into a uniformed marching band."

How many passions have been lost to students who were told their natural aptitudes were leading them in the "wrong" direction, and whose talents were blunted by the corporate-approved drive toward regimented conformity?

Besides teaching this hidden curriculum, Gallo asserts, the schools also separate children from their families, thereby weakening the bonds of family. This attack against the family is a part of the larger campaign in America to atomize people into individuals, so that having only themselves, they are weak and helpless and unable to resist the establishment, Johmann notes.

Having read this laundry list of what public schools do to our children, isn't it clear that our government is behaving in the same way as our monolithic school system, and isn't it even clearer that this process is not producing thoughtful human beings? Instead, the vast majority are the flag-waving zombies who cheer as American military might murders innocent children in faraway places, and turns its own citizens into robotic, thoughtless advocates of "the war on terror"?

If you have kids in school, be sure and study Johmann's website and its links before you make the decision to get them out of public schools as fast as you possibly can.

14

How we lost our freedom

9/11 and JFK: An American lament

We let them get away with it.

And that's why they keep doing what they do.

When the powers that be were allowed to proclaim, forty years ago, that the murder of John F. Kennedy was the work of a lone gunman—a conclusion virtually no one ever believed—the American people sent a signal to their leaders that they could basically get away with anything they wanted, and the people would not significantly—and certainly not effectively—object.

What followed, as we all know, has been a litany of murderous deception: the downed airliners ruled accidents, the massacre of children and mothers holding babies, and the cynical demolition of American landmarks that were blamed on mysterious but unidentified (or misidentified) terrorists, for whom new repressive laws were instantly (and suspiciously) enacted.

Now the World Trade Center has come and gone, the fragments of what was once the world's tallest buildings are buried in secrecy, and still no legitimate investigation into how this incomprehensible tragedy happened has been undertaken, never mind concluded.

The message could not be clearer: the people who have obstructed a probe into 9/11 are the ones who benefit from obstructing it, and quite likely the ones who dreamed up the whole thing in the first place.

This tragic fact has been more or less verified with the recent revelation that the Project for a New American Century, a gang of Republican (and Zionist) warmongers, wrote a paper in 2000 advising that America needed a "Pearl Harbor type event" in order to justify the creation of new laws to limit freedom, and thereby improve conditions for increased business banditry by the very rich. Yet this is a notion that the mass media, which are wholly owned by many of the same interests who benefited from the 9/11 attacks, will never admit, never mind write about.

When an event happens that has been recommended by someone as desirable to happen, the people who made the recommendation in the first place should become the prime suspects. But that has not happened in America, which brags it is a free country, but never seems to get the truth about the truly momentous events in its own history.

Why? Because we let them get away with it.

We have let President Bush II win the debate day with such senseless pronouncements as "the terrorists hate our freedom" and allowed him to murder 5,000 innocent people in Afghanistan without a shred of evidence that any of them were involved in the tragedies in New York and Washington. We have allowed America to be surreally twisted into a hateful place where suspects are now guilty until proven innocent, without applying the same criteria to the actual perpetrators of the violence who manipulate and distort the social and political agenda to their own profitable aims.

And it's too late to fix the situation. Let's face it. They got away with it. It's water over the dam, old news. There's no going back now. The die is cast. The dead are buried. The facts are firmly covered up. New crises now distract us.

There is one positive factor that has come out of all this death and deception: people are taking a harder look at American history. Some are realizing that what is happening today has been happening all along.

We've harped on and lamented plenty about the criminal destruction of the American Indians. So for those young adults new to serious criticism of America's bloody and imperialist history, let's start with the Philippines and the so-called Spanish American War in 1898–99. The Philippines drove the Spanish out on their own, but then the Americans decided those strategically placed islands were too lucrative to pass up and proceeded to kill 1.5 million Filipinos, while all the time the American people were reading in their own newspapers that the U.S. was helping these poor islanders fight the Spanish and "rebels." The phrase "war on terror" had not yet been invented, but the meaning was the same, more than a century ago. The war on terror is a war on freedom.

World Wars I and II were essentially started by the West as Germany got too strong economically. Regardless of what you may have read in the schools that try to shape your mind on orders from the power elite, it was the machinations of Britain and the U.S. that essentially squeezed Germany and Japan into economic depressions that they tried to shoot their way out of. This is the very strategy now being used by the United States with its trumped up rationale about the need to attack Iraq.

Let's cut to the contemporary chase and jump to 1963. Kennedy had fired CIA chief Allen Dulles after the Bay of Pigs fiasco. Dulles, of course, along with Nixon and Bush, were the prime players in a continuous effort to destabilize the American economy by creating wars to stimulate arms-production profits. They were the prime players in a group of seriously rich industrialists who had financed Adolf Hitler in order to make money off the creation of the war known as The Big One. Allen Dulles, you may remember, was later named to head the Warren Commission that determined the assassination was the work of a lone nut.

Lone nuts were also falsely blamed for the murders of Martin Luther King Jr. and Bobby Kennedy. These too were stories that were never widely believed, but allowed to stand by the disoriented and deluded American populace.

The justification for the Vietnam war, triggered by a totally fictional incident, was similarly preposterous, trying to stop the

Communist domino effect, according to the American papers, while in reality Ho Chi Minh had been asking for American help against the Chinese since World War I. In 1947, Ho again wrote a letter to Truman, expressing admiration for the U.S. and asking for assistance against the Chinese and the French. Truman never answered him, a decision that was to cost millions of lives two decades later. But that didn't matter. The profits of Dow and Dupont were all that did matter.

In recent years, buoyed by all these triumphs of deception, the atrocities became more frequent and more profound. I love these clowns who say the American government would never kill its own citizens. American history is chock full of examples in which the U.S. government has eagerly obliterated its own, especially its own military personnel (think Gulf War vaccines and Agent Orange) but also its average citizens (think, most recently, AIDS and anthrax).

In the 1990s, with foreign wars in relatively short supply, the focus of the beast turned inward, with the first WTC attack, Ruby Ridge, Waco, and Oklahoma City events all fomented from within the bowels of the American intelligence apparatus.

The first WTC bombing included a plant among the duped Egyptian terrorists who urged his controllers not to let the attack go forward when there was a clear opportunity to stop it, but the FBI let it happen anyway. More convincing that way.

At that small cabin in Idaho, the man who approved of a sniper putting a bullet in the forehead of a young mother holding her baby was later given a medal and appointed to be assistant director of the FBI.

And why did Janet Reno give the order to burn babies at Waco merely over some theological disputation? Why did the feds say they didn't know why Flight 800 blew up when, so far, 757 people have come forward to say they saw missiles hit the plane? Why did they insist JFK, Jr. was a bad pilot? These were all lies, and we knew it. But we let them get away with it.

Prior to 9/11, my favorite preposterous atrocity explanation involved the government's demolition of the Murrah building in

Oklahoma. Esteemed General Benton K. Partin delivered an incontrovertible report that explosives attached to five major stanchions inside the building were responsible for bringing the building down, and killing 168, but his expert testimony was ignored and the blame was placed directly on where the power elite intended it to be placed, on American patriots. Of course, the anti-terror legislation had already been written then, too, and was quickly passed with little debate.

And now we come to the watershed event in American history, 9/11, which precipitated the virtual suspension of the U.S. Constitution, because a Republican think tank had written several years before the event happened that this would be a profitable idea.

More than a year after this latest tragedy, no rational explanation has been presented to the American people, only charges without evidence and stilted and implausible cover stories tossed around that were quickly shot full of holes. And more murders. Lots more murders.

The deceitful deed has been covered up in the same way that all those other dirty deeds have always been covered up, with more manipulated events to distract everyone's attention and new crises to drive the "old" stories from the newspapers.

The anthrax attacks, almost surely carried out by government provocateurs, were meant to convince us that the "terrorist" crisis was continuing, and hypervigilance was required. Then, when the business histories of Bush and his demonic vice president threatened to blow up in their faces, a war against the innocent people of Iraq was fomented, despite rationales that elicited nothing but laughter and scorn from around the world.

In all of these situations, we let them get away with it. As a people, we did not and do not have the power, the clout, the impact, to overturn what our "elected" representatives perpetrate upon us. We have been taught to be sheep, not to rock the boat, not to challenge authority, not to question the official version of events lest our paydays be interrupted. We relinquish freedom for bribes.

As we have abandoned justice for the people of this planet, these are our 30 pieces of silver.

And now there's nothing we can do except go to the prison camps they send us to and take the poisons they prescribe for us, because we were always afraid to jeopardize our paltry paychecks and say the things we really felt, and make those things stick. This is how the American people forfeited freedom for the entire world.

15

The shadow of her smile

How we are responsible for the evil that enslaves us . . . and what to do about it

> *"In times of change, learners inherit the earth, while the learned find themselves beautifully equipped to deal with a world that no longer exists."*
>
> —Eric Hoffer

I used to love fireworks. But I haven't been able to watch them for better than a decade now, ever since that first time, lying in a pristine field in a small country town, when I looked up at the pretty colors in the night sky and imagined, unmistakably, that what I was hearing were the screams of dying Iraqi children.

Sometimes when I'm shaving that part of my face I don't call my beard, I'll catch a face in the mirror; not mine, but down in the corner of my eye, an image will stop me from what I'm doing. It's a fleeting face, tiny and indistinct. I'll look more closely and it will be gone. But it will linger in my memory, and I've come to think of those hallucinated faces as the lives our American prosperity is built on, living people we never knew whose lives were tossed away in an anonymous cauldron of carnage in some faraway place we seldom hear about.

How many times have we said it: "America is the greatest country in the world." And it is. Everything is just perfect . . . if we don't contemplate the unknown horror and unreported violence upon which our paradise is built.

William Blum, author of *Rogue State* and chronicler of American depredations throughout the world, estimates the U.S. has killed seven million innocent people since World War II. Most people don't stop and think how we get what we have, where all this opulence comes from.

So I go back to shaving, but now, as long I live, and because of what I know, the smile on the face staring back at me contains a shadow I dread to see again.

• • •

Many of us who read such skeptical underground publications as *Paranoia, American Free Press* or *From the Wilderness* don't really need to be updated about the latest lies our leaders tell us, although God knows they come at us faster than we can handle them. We've made it our business to know what's going on behind the headlines and consequently can perceive the avalanche of falsehoods that camouflages the endless robbery of the poor by the rich and the damage these demonic fictions do to our planet and its inhabitants.

Yet the lies and wars and phony justifications continue from one generation to the next, and no amount of investigative reporting—no matter how accurate or shocking—seems to be able to change the behavior of that warped family of aristocratic human predators who have taken control of the way we think and behave. This control enables them to say and do what they want, and the people of the world—distracted by their more mundane concerns like children and paychecks—continue to be afflicted by the schemes of the powerful, with no measure of supposedly democratic participation able to derail this pathological parade of lethal greed that now threatens to make our planet completely uninhabitable.

The two primary mechanisms that keep ordinary Americans distracted from these schemes of tyranny are the schools and the media. A third mechanism, which I shall deal with later, is religion, and the sacred approval these hypocritical institutions have provided to mass murderers throughout history.

But for now, as we face the new police-state threat foisted on us by the George W. Bush gang and its predecessors, the two primary vehicles that allow the powers that be to remain largely invisible and unaccountable as they plunder the planet and enslave its residents seem to be the schools, which in the past century have become little more than programs to teach people not to question authority, and the media, which are owned by the same rich men who create the wars and sell the weapons that make them fabulously wealthy.

If you accept this argument, the solution becomes obvious: change the schools from indoctrination programs that create well-dressed day laborers to genuine educational institutions that produce thoughtful philosophers, and detach the media from the rich criminals who own them. I know, I know: easier said than done. And maybe impossible.

A logical first step in beginning the process of reclaiming our schools and our media as nontoxic members of our society is recognizing the phenomenon known as corporate personhood. In 1886, the Supreme Court of the United States issued an edict that was as damaging to human freedom as its 2000 ruling to make Bush II the president. The infamous Santa Clara decision gave corporations the same rights as humans, whereas prior to that, corporations had to be chartered by the states, they couldn't own other unrelated businesses that weren't included in their original charter, and these charters could be revoked if the corporations engaged in bad behavior. Just imagine: if corporations were criminals, their charters were taken away and their assets liquidated.

How much human misery could have been averted if those laws had remained in effect?

But they didn't. Just like today, judges and senators were bribed and the measure eventually passed without even any debate. Ever since, American citizens have been the powerless subjects of big business fat cats, and communities have been destroyed by tycoons who make criminal decisions from far away.

Currently, two major organizations are working to bring this issue to public consciousness: Reclaim Democracy (http://www.reclaimdemocracy.org/) and POCLAD (Program on Corporations, Law and Democracy, (http://www.poclad.org/). Their efforts are still patchwork and their objectives are still a little fuzzy in the public mind, but they share the aim of taking away the real power in our country and the world from soulless corporations and returning that power to people with consciences. It could be done legislatively if our elected representatives were not so corrupt.

What kind of world do we want? Do we want the best possible products or the best possible communities? The highest possible profits or the best possible lives for all humans? I urge all of you to investigate this matter more carefully, but I realize what we're up against in regard to getting such measures as restarting the corporate charter system through our criminal legislatures. Therefore, what is needed are ballot initiatives to overturn the 1886 Santa Clara decision and begin to return ultimate power to ordinary people in an actualized democracy.

However, we face another complicating factor before we can address the corporate personhood issue: electronic voting. The recent implementation of Touchscreen voting machines in most states poses the single biggest current threat to our freedom. These machines are all owned by political operatives, who by computer manipulation can change any vote total at any time.

Plenty of evidence of this surfaced in the 2002 elections, and a national movement is growing to outlaw all computer voting machines, because no one can adequately audit the vote totals. A truly honest country would invalidate the entire 2002 election because of this, but we know what the score is, and unless all of these machines can be eliminated, all hope for a legitimate democracy and an honest vote count are gone. For more information on this and other aspects of vote manipulation, check out http://www.talion.com.

And even if this were accomplished, the lack of a legitimate opposition party in the United States all but guarantees the destructive practices of the power elite cannot be thwarted in the foreseeable future. Consider the current Democratic candidates lining up to oppose Bush in the 2004 election: Skull & Bones cultist John Kerry and Zionists Hillary Clinton and Joe Lieberman. So even if this new electronic vote scam is fixed, the candidates of the power elite will assure that nothing will change, and the slide toward oblivion for the planet and economic enslavement for ordinary people will continue.

Still, we cannot but try to at least restore some degree of integrity to our voting system.

Once voting is again conducted with pencils on paper ballots (it's the most honest way, and used all over Europe) and the corporate personhood issue has been resolved in favor of actual people, then we can begin to deal with the totalitarian problems of schools aimed to create robots and all the newspapers and TV stations owned by that small circle of billionaire thugs.

Currently, schools are headed in the wrong direction, with all sorts of corporate incentives being dangled in front of cash-strapped school districts and teachers. Polluting industries besiege teachers at conventions, twisting facts to get teachers to tell their students global warming is a fallacy. Huge agribusiness throws money at schools to teach that pesticides and biotech foods are good things. Schools sell space to advertisers and as a result receive unhealthy products for free. And now, so-called faith-based initiatives threaten to erase the last vestige of progressive ideas from our less fortunate neighborhoods and replace them with a corrupt series of discriminatory control mechanisms ruled over by morally bankrupt fundamentalist Christian zealots.

If you've watched TV lately, the environment and the common person have no defenders. A one-sided stream of pseudo-patriotic invective glorifies the lies of George Bush and treats each fictional claim about Iraq's threat as being beyond question. Then, when the pro-war public relations gimmicks are one-by-one exposed as lies, they are buried at the bottom of newscasts as incidental corrections.

No one person should own more than one newspaper, or one TV station.

In fact, no one should own any property they don't live on. (A humane society of the future will pass that law, if the human race regains control of itself.) But on TV, owned by the same masters who make the weapons and the drugs, no one talks about any of that.

Beginning with A.S. Neill and his famous school and book, *Summerhill*, all compassionate and honest educators have known that the best educational system is one chosen by the children, and not one determined by psychologists or drug companies. Currently, most objective observers describe today's schools as being driven by the forces of marketing, as multinationals try to brainwash our children into becoming brand-loyal consumers.

School officials have notoriously sold out to the forces of capitalism in exchange for big salaries, and most conscientious parents with the financial wherewithal to choose alternatives no longer send their children to public schools. Many teachers betray their primary missions by focusing on the authority of their teaching rather than the genuine needs of the children being educated. Teachers have been brainwashed, too, and seek to impose that brainwashing on their unwitting pupils.

A child free to choose individual courses of study—and we all want to be educated; no child, given a choice, would choose not to be educated—will become an adult demanding accurate news reports, not like now, when all kids are hammered into the same trendy molds, riddled with drugs and corporate-concocted music, and expected to partake in the same lockstep media crap that now afflicts us all. No wonder they rebel and shoot guns at their peers!

So if the school problem could be fixed, the media problem would take care of itself. Politicians would no longer be able to say they couldn't reveal certain information because of national security, because all people would be intimately involved with the security and progress of their own nation or state.

The only reason government officials seek to keep details of their deals secret is not for national security but because their rich friends are making money off the deals they cloak in righteous, patriotic rhetoric. Throughout history, it has always been this way. The public just never catches up with that realization, because, victims of inferior education that they are, they are overwhelmed by the phony stories, and by neighbors who have been bribed to support the scams, convincing skeptics not to rock the boat in the name of patriotism.

Imagine a really intelligent person who had created and achieved her own educational goals having to choose from the ridiculously delusional media spectrum of today, where everything is aimed toward duping consumers into buying products they don't really need. Truly educated people would all simply stop reading and listening to the false information now perpetrated on Fox, CNN and Clear Channel Radio. These bad acts would go out of business in a heartbeat.

All the colleges would fail, too, because they now try to do the same thing as the public schools—try to hammer disparate personalities into pre-packaged slots to create more effective worker bees and unquestioning consumers. Even the medical professions suffer from this rigid regimentation, and the public suffers as less popular but more relevant medical treatments are shut out by curricula determined by commercial interests rather than healers with integrity. That's why the doctors give everybody so many drugs—it's profitable and better yet (for them), no one ever gets well.

OK, let's review so far. The mainstream media are our big problem (not because they're too right or too left; those are phony distinctions designed to distract you) because they don't ever tell you what's really going on. They don't tell you the U.S. is in Colombia to smooth the flow of drugs to the international cartels; they say America is there to stop the flow of drugs to street dealers. They don't tell you American soldiers beat people to death in the streets of Colombia simply for growing up in the wrong neighborhood, either. But it happens, a lot more often than you would like to believe (and in many other countries, too, from Panama to Bosnia).

The mainstream media are never going to tell you that the U.S. government created AIDS at Fort Detrick, Maryland, because they make far too much money accepting advertising from the pharmaceutical giants who helped implement that program to ever reveal a truth so close to home.

You seldom hear about the Bush family's connections to either Adolf Hitler or Osama bin Laden—or that these so-called al-Qaeda terrorists were funded by the U.S. and their Saudi co-conspirators because, well, that wouldn't be patriotic! Instead they hammer out lie after lie beneath logos blaring "Showdown with Iraq" without mentioning that all the stated rationales for such a rash excursion are out-and-out falsehoods, unprovable assertions designed only to aid in the flow of cash to the rich men who make the guns, the radioactive waste, and the prescription drugs.

I could go on about this; most of you already know the score. What is really needed is a wider circulation of the perceptions many of us already have to those less informed, less worldly, with less access to the independent, underground web media that try so hard to dispel the myths that distract us.

We need to talk about the 9/11 questions in a rational manner: why the air defenses didn't react, why Bush went to that school and talked to children for a half hour even though he knew two planes had attacked New York, why so many people were tipped off not to fly on that fateful day. This outreach is essential to have a larger audience questioning the fictions about 9/11, Enron and other noteworthy corporate crimes that now are not being adequately addressed.

The amazing thing about talking to people who haven't had access to a lot of the revealing details about recent political events that are now found on the Internet is that they tend to already know, intuitively, what you're saying. Most people know the media polls have been lying all along; Bush is ridiculous. If his level of evolution were the level of American culture, we wouldn't even have invented the car yet.

Everybody, in their own way, knows that something is profoundly wrong with today's American society. It's just a matter of those having the information at their disposal disseminating it effectively. You also have to weed out, or avoid, those who have been paid off to maintain a pro-establishment point of view either by political entities or religious organizations. There are a lot of moles out there, who will string you along for awhile before revealing their true objectives, whether members of the impotent Democratic party, cynical Christian schools or deceptive Zionist apologists (sometimes, you get three in one). These three groups are working against the improvement of society in favor of their own narrow-minded goals, which often they don't really believe themselves but have been talked into believing because of their guilt over not really understanding what is truly going on.

Which leads us to the most important aspect of our current dilemma—the matter of religion, specifically, the killer religions: Christianity, Judaism, and Islam. Adherents of each demonize the other two, claiming their version of God is the infallible one, even though all three derive from the same teachings, known as the Torah or the Pentateuch (first five books of the Old Testament), and even have the same founder, Abraham.

Up until the present day, devotees of these religions are the greatest murderers of human beings in history. Members of each religion are currently prominent in most of the major political conflicts of the present day. It is probably disingenuous to insist that these religions are the causes of current conflicts—because the politicians who determine wars' causes exploit religion, they don't practice it. But it is undeniable that religions provide the behavioral groundwork for practitioners of these "holy" rites to indulge in the mass murder of their opposition. So in that sense, they do bear a fundamental responsibility for the continuing violence, in that they all condone the slaughter of innocents as a legitimate redress for their real or trumped-up grievances.

I bring this up for the purpose of pointing out that without these holy orders to kill from the most respected teachers in each of these religions, we likely would not have the intensity of political conflicts that now cause us so much tragedy. Sure, the stated reasons of most of these conflicts involve commodities like oil, but the political rhetoric that finally triggers them is inevitably couched in terms and concepts we learned from our holy books.

We scapegoat others for behavior that we ourselves practice. As the old saying goes, one person's terrorist is another person's freedom fighter. In religious terms, the holy killing of our enemies makes us feel more alive, which is really why the killing happens in the first place.

Very few people can as yet see that the lie we tell ourselves about eternal life is directly related to war. Belief in an afterlife cheapens life on this planet. And from this epiphany comes the explanation of why Bush is so popular among those who do not think deeply, and why so many of us want this war—want any war—because it makes us feel more secure in some primitive, unexamined way.

As the little known cultural anthropologist Ernest Becker pointed out, the evil men produce derives from the very heroism they seek to achieve. We seek to achieve this heroism because it insulates us from the terror of death; it gives us a reason to live in an otherwise meaningless world. Death denial—a.k.a. the belief in an afterlife—allows us to live comfortably but makes us practice rituals of destruction, and from this destruction, we derive pleasure and justification for our sad little lives.

As the world's multifaceted environmental crisis intensifies—the oceans are poisoned, the air is fouled, half of all animal species have disappeared since the start of the Industrial Age, and global warming threatens to soon change the face of our landmass—the time has definitely come in human history to question all of our behavior, especially that supernatural religious propaganda that not only allows us to kill everything in sight—but praises us for doing it in defense of senseless, ephemeral and deluded goals.

I wouldn't go so far as to blame God for all these problems. I would lay the problem squarely at the feet of our priests, who were always supposed to tell us how to live justly but who have really only shown us how to kill without guilt.

If we could begin to fix this problem, I have a hunch a lot of the other, lesser problems would evaporate, because then we would be living lives of true compassion and justice. And as long as we worship a jealous, vengeful God who urges us on to the glorious slaughter of our enemies, peace is simply not going to happen, and we are truly doomed to live out our lives with increasing levels of mass murder, pollution, and meaninglessness.

• • •

As I look in the mirror, I see that all this is my fault, as much as anybody else's. The world has been pretty much destroyed on my watch, in my lifetime. In 1974 when I first woke up to the lies of Nixon and the shameless charade in Vietnam, sure, I got out and waved my signs. But like so many others, I couldn't identify the clearly evident sociological patterns of exploitation and destruction that I have described herein. They existed then as well as now. But I hid my head, pursued my trivial desires, and hoped somebody would fix this mess. Nobody did.

I wouldn't care all that much now, because I don't have too many days left on this planet, except that when I look in the mirror to shave, down in the corner of my eye, I see, fleetingly, this little girl's face. An imaginary construct, no doubt, etched in my memory from some Save the Children ad on TV. A little girl with a dirty face, smiling, but long dead, bludgeoned to death by some Guatemalan death squad working for a coffee plantation billionaire, or napalmed from 30,000 feet in Vietnam, or decayed to death in Iraq after playing with her doll in some depleted uranium dirt. She was killed unnoticed by the American war machine, the same evil entity that now prepares to do more of the same in virtually every country on Earth.

It is this little, unnoticed face that American prosperity is built upon. It happened in my lifetime, right before my eyes. Her smile is the shadow in my heart.

• • •

Relevant reference material:

> Two books by the cultural anthropologist Ernest Becker (1924-74): *The Denial of Death and Escape from Evil,* explain, among other things that "war is a sociological safety valve that cleverly diverts popular hatred for ruling classes into a happy occasion to mutilate or kill foreign enemies" and that "killing others lessens our own fear of dying, although it is our own sense of animality and inferiority we try to kill—and never succeed."
>
> Summerhill: The first school in England where inspectors must use the children's opinions in the evaluation of the school: http://www.s-hill.demon.co.uk.

16

Collect call from Planet X

Do you really want to know who's on the line?

Operator: "You have a collect call from Planet X. Will you accept the charges?

Me: "Duh . . . who's calling? And what do they want?"

Oh, come on! You've heard about Planet X. It's the new successor to the Y2K song-and-dance, another excuse to stock up on canned goods and change the curtains in the bomb shelter. Planet X, according to a hysterical spate of popular books and articles, is a celestial body some say is three times the size of Jupiter about to devastate the Earth with its gravitational chaos and cause apocalyptic "earth changes" and a "pole shift," and make lots of money for these New Age gurus preaching the ever-popular specter of agonizing apocalypse—urging you to buy their long-lasting batteries.

I think it noteworthy that as organized religion has declined in a sordid soup of sex abuse scandals and embarrassing political entanglements—not to mention embezzlement, terror and murder—the ET industry has correspondingly prospered. What is it about this sad human race that we need something invisible and fantastic to cling to, especially if it dangles us over the edge of death and destruction?

But is it real? you ask. Is Planet X really the threat to our existence some people say?

I don't even know if it's worth the time to discuss this at all . . . except that there seems to be a shadowy psychological connection between the myths people choose to believe and what really happens in the actual world. It's not so much that our wildest wishes have a bearing on the outcome of actions (although this is true in some cases). Rather, what we bring down on ourselves is often a case of what we had hoped for is then developed by others as a commercial opportunity, an exploitable way to make a quick buck or two, usually to the detriment of all but the concocter.

That's how churches got started, isn't it? As magical rituals to anesthetize our fear of death. It's the same principle fundamentalist Christians use today to support Israeli Zionists while they secretly hope their support triggers Armageddon (which will wipe out all those unrepentant Zionists who are now their allies) as God shows up in his shiny Starship New Jerusalem to spirit away the faithful—the Chosen—to that great RV in the sky, which presumably is parked in the same lot as Planet X.

It also happens in the geopolitical world, say, when a certain dark-skinned minority is totally set up and blamed for some colossal catastrophe that results in thousands of badly educated yahoos driving around in their pickup trucks looking to waste the first raghead they can find.

The truly dangerous aspect of all this is that people who choose to believe in an impending menace from outer space are, by my reckoning, many of the very same people who accept the same killer myths that threaten our survival, that the Middle East conflict is about some Book of Revelation curse rather than the mundane scam about land and money that it surely is.

• • •

Is a great horror from outer space merely an excuse, just a way to divert our attention from our own shortcomings, our own crimes, our own guilt? Or, as the true believers would have us believe, is it some strange species knowledge of what happened once before and will happen again?

I've seen members of this latter group marking off the days on their Mayan calendars, counting down to December 21, 2012, when the big "galactic synchronization" is supposed to occur, the end of the 25,000-year Mayan great cycle.

Is speculation on events so far away that if we traveled all our lives at speeds faster than we have ever reached, we still couldn't reach them . . . are these subjects akin to religion, constructed to delude us into forgetting that one day all of us will shed this mortal coil and leave behind nothing but our reputations? To put that more clearly, does contemplating the death of our species or our planet somehow give us comfort in deflecting us from thinking about our own personal imminent demise, which some people insist is the true objective of all social behavior?

Or is this persistent fantasy of catastrophic death from above actually a legitimate—and evolving—astronomical syndrome that could have more impact on human history than any other single previous event?

I mean, what DID take out those dinosaurs 65 million years ago?

Through the time machine in our minds comes Ronald Reagan's famous contemplation of peace: "I occasionally think how quickly our differences, worldwide, would vanish if we were facing an alien threat from outside this world."

And in the newsreel of our memories flash the Fatima prophecies, Orson Welles' "War of the Worlds" broadcast, the enduring Roswell sideshow and those enigmatic lights in the sky, not to mention the movie *E.T.* and that paleontology book with the classic title, *T. Rex and the Crater of Doom.*

Most perusals on matters involving outer space, lately—if they're not activities astronomers can prove are legitimate celestial events, such as the Hale Bopp or Shoemaker Levy comets, which everyone could see—have been relegated to bookstores with crystals and dragons that are frequented by middle-aged women in long skirts.

In that latter category—commonly called the New Age—a legend has grown up over the past 20 years about a mystery planet, sometimes called "Nemesis" or "Nibiru," attended by arcane biblical references and fantasies of super-intelligent space travelers. The most popular of these, the ten or so books in Zecharia Sitchin's *War in Heaven* series, have been so popular they have spawned second- and third-generation imitators and propelled the prehistoric culture of Sumer (an ancient geographical region now generally known as Iraq) to a never-anticipated popularity.

They are also the basis of the latest Planet X craze, whether today's imitators say so or not.

None of these books, Sitchin's or anybody else's, has ever passed the science test, in the minds of the vast majority of qualified readers. Sitchin's depictions of prehistoric Mesopotamian culture are riddled with bad footnotes, spurious mistranslations and grievous physics errors that have utterly ruined his chances for scientific credibility, though these faults have not diminished his popularity among legions of would-be believers. A little pseudoscience goes a long way in the minds of P.T. Barnum's target audience. (You remember the famous quote: "Nobody ever lost a dime underestimating the intelligence of the American public.")

The gross financial product of so many Sitchinesque websites, books, support groups, channelers and debunkers has reached considerable proportions, the champ of which category today appears to be a $50 book by one Mark Hazlewood called *Blindsided: Planet X Passes in 2003*. That's right. Get those batteries ready.

There are many other would-be luminaries on this astral bandwagon that I won't mention here. For a look at all this outer space snake oil, I highly recommend Phil Plait's "Bad Astronomy" web page (http://www.badastronomy.com/bad/misc/planetx/index.html)if you wish to immerse (and detox) yourself in the latest apocalyptic elixirs of a most dubious nature.

As with Sitchin (and his apostles Alford, Horne and Icke), this latest posse of poseurs could just as easily be swept away with an irritated wave of the hand, except for one small thing . . . the number of people who, believing in such questionable disciplines as astrology, spirit contact, and the power of crystals, represents no small percentage of the population. And then the question becomes, again in the minds of those believers, if they believe it will happen does that mean it WILL happen?

There are two ways to become a promoter of the Planet X myth. One road runs through science that implies just an intriguing hint of spirit, while the other road meanders through the highly subjective impulses of spirit and is sweetened by just enough science to get the faithful to conclude they can't understand the subject without appealing to a higher power.

Let's dispatch the spiritual approach first because it is so transparently absurd. Let's consider the urgent communiqués of one Christos Lightweaver, which came in by e-mail today and insists:

> What is known for sure is that a large "Planet X" comet is coming in from behind the sun. (As if something could hide behind the sun.) It is being covered up/blacked-out by the controlled media but SOHO photos on the web by independent astrophysicists show it to be highly magnetic and already causing massive solar corona ejecta when it passed between Venus and the Sun. When it passes the earth it could do the same, attracting solar ejecta with effects ranging from scorching "fire from the sky" to massive lightening [sic] storms and EMP pulses. It could also trigger the pole shift with 300 mile per hour winds, mile high tidal waves, massive earthquakes and unprecedented volcanism creating a "nuclear winter" effect (extreme cold) for years to come."

Mr. Lightweaver attempts to appear empirically reasonable by saying: "On top of that, we've had so many disaster movies the last several years that people have been inoculated (desensitized) against the real thing." He says it's a brown dwarf star, quotes Hazlewood, and attaches himself to the post 9/11 political disquiet that is now sweeping the land. He attributes the global economic meltdown, politically expedient terror, and even quotes the recently canonized Padre Pio as sure indications that Planet X is bearing down on us, as he pathetically grasps for support with helpings of buzzwords from any discipline that catches his attention.

In addition, he borrows huge handfuls of Sitchin's mythology to support his arguments: Reptilian Anunnaki replicants are now among us, an alien super race. There are those who believe that the Anunnaki of Nibiru are coming back to Earth soon. They believe that Planet X is going to pass by Earth, in May or June of 2003, on its 3,600 year orbit around our sun. Such believers are terrified of the consequences that a close pass by Nibiru might bring. They fear this will cause earthquakes, tidal waves, severe flooding, food shortages due to climatic conditions, diseases, meteor fire storms, volcanic eruptions and the like. They are afraid that it will result in a great catastrophic infliction of loss of life on Earth.

Mr. Lightweaver also notes that Anunnaki civilization is also "interspersed in the Orion and Pleiades systems." This statement is a sure sign of a charlatan.

I love it when people do this, because they can't even figure out that constellations as seen from Earth are like pictures on a wall; they are in no way groups of stars in three dimensions because the stars comprising each constellation are all at varying distances from Earth, some much farther from each other than they are from Earth. So anytime anybody uses phrases like Pleiadians, Arcturians, or the name of any other constellations, you know they're huckster idiots, despite the often alluring nature of their earthbound political commentary. Some of the best socialist political commentary I've ever read came from Commander Hatonn, once a prominent Pleiadian strategist based in Las Vegas.

Oh, yes, Mr. Lightweaver has one other piece of advice for you during the passage of Planet X, which he believes has been brought down on us by the nefarious influences of the Anunnaki agents still on Earth.

What is it?

"Target the forces of Anunnaki anti-love with your Ruby Rayguns."

OK. Beyond stupid. But I'm sure he's making lots of money with this shtick. I wonder if you can get Ruby Rayguns at Wal-mart, yet?

Let's address the pseudoscientific approach, which is somewhat more realistic and alluring, as long as you don't look under the illogical rocks littering the trail.

NASA groupie Richard Hoagland reached Sitchin's class of compelling New Age vaudevillians when he convinced millions that "the face on Mars" was actually a vestige of a once-great civilization that actually lived there. Fortunately, recent NASA photos have revealed the thing for what it is—a hill with a few creases in it.

But like true hoaxers throughout history, Hoagland has moved on to bigger and better stuff, and occupies a prominent position in the new Planet X hootenanny with a brilliantly constructed sleight-of-mind explanation that attempts to utilize the new and fuzzy disciplines of hyperdimensional physics, so-called scalar electromagnetics and celestial mechanics.

To make a long and involved story short, Hoagland insists that by using hyperdimensional geometric indicators that he himself discovered on Mars, which led to a new appreciation of the lost physics revelations of 18th century scientist James Clerk Maxwell, called questionable quarternions, plus a photograph indicating a planet spit out of its own solar system by twin suns, plus the as-yet unverified tendency of some planets to emit their own heat, plus a little dose of hyperdimensional physics espoused by Michio Kaku, plus a heaping helping of the scalar electromagnetic theories of Thomas Bearden, plus the insistence that modern physicists just don't get it, plus the discovery that hyperdimensional stress energy indicates our solar system's planets affect the angular momentum of our Sun much more than previously thought—all indicate that an unknown planet exists, a Jovian-type (that means like Jupiter) exists some 450 light years from the Sun.

That, as they say, is pretty far out, since a good 20 known stars exist within 20 light years of our Sun.

Of course, the dimensions in his formula are experimentally unreachable (they certainly are), but through his dedicated research, he has discovered that great secret that there is in fact a Planet X-type heavenly body bearing down on us.

Sigh. As web critic Michael Goodspeed has noted, (http://-www.ufowatchdog.com/hoagie.html) Hoagland has claimed to be the discoverer of numerous "firsts" in the outer space: glass structures on the moon, oceans on Europa, a signal from a spaceship in the constellation Pegasus (which was supposed to have arrived some years ago), fake asteroids sent by ETs to warn us of real asteroids, and underground cities on Mars (http://www. macton-nies.com/imperative34.html). Goodspeed concludes, "Of all the questionable characters on the alternative scene today, perhaps none has been accused of such indiscretions more often than

Richard C. Hoagland." And it is Hoagland who has constructed the most believable scenario about Planet X.

Now, I said all that to say this.

When you get that collect call from Planet X—when some utterly sincere individual attempts to apprise you of the hottest new details of this latest apocalyptic threat to life on Earth—just hang up the phone. It's just another cold call from someone who couldn't master the facts if he had them, trying to sell you something you don't need.

Wake up! Nothing that is 450 light years away is going to be here sooner than 450 years. Get it?

What really fries my frijoles is when one of these "channelers" tries to lump together current political events with these supposedly current celestial "events," because all that does is demean and discredit all the hard work put in by thousands of honest researchers who have been trying to tell you something is wrong with the current political picture that has been presented by our completely corrupted mass media.

When these two subjects are connected, both become bogus. But the fact is, one of these scenarios—the one taking place on Earth—is very real, while the other—taking place "out there"—is definitely a paranoid fantasy to delude the public for the purpose of making money off the easily gullible, which now that I think of it is very similar to President Bush's paranoid fantasy that it is right and honorable to use a totally false story to seize another country's oil fields. If anything is true, maybe it's that President Bush is really the Planet X about to bring apocalypse to the whole world, and if we're focusing on some imaginary, mythological threat from outer space, chances are good we won't see the impending disaster that is right now on our doorstep.

All these trendy rumblings about Planet X are merely the echoes of our own mortality. It is the echo of our own guilt for destroying a planet that, except for the presence of the human species, remains perfectly lovely and quite likely is the most hospitable place in the entire universe.

The possibility that in the late spring of this year we are about to be obliterated by a large invader from space is not real, and not worth a moment of our further study. The probability that babies are about to be obliterated by laser-guided, depleted-uranium bombs dropped from American fighter jets IS real, and deserves every waking moment of our most profound attention.

P.S.: A prominent ET channeler website insists all the above-mentioned players (except Mr. Lightweaver) are agents of one government or another, specifically tasked to foul the playing field for legitimate investigators in the fields of celestial mechanics and scalar electromagnetics. Although I put no stock in channelers, I'd have to agree with their assertion that these channeled entities occasionally tell the truth when it suits their purposes.

17

The system can't be fixed

Our future is a dark age of vicious guards and powerless prisoners

Our president is a criminal and if not surely guilty, at least chargeable for the following offenses:

- Military desertion
- Cocaine smuggling
- Conspiracy to destroy American landmarks
- Conspiracy to commit mass murder in New York, Washington, Pennsylvania and Afghanistan.
- Treason, for sure.
- Willful and deliberate destruction of the U.S. Constitution.
- Accessory to the theft of billions of dollars in the savings and loan debacle engineered and/or condoned by his father.
- Corruption for making repeated and continuing governmental decisions to enrich his relatives and friends.
- Obstruction of justice, innumerable counts, for blocking investigations into crimes that cost the lives of thousands of American citizens.

- Kidnapping and torture, for putting thousands of innocent people in jail without trial and denying them their constitutional rights, as well as killing some. Illegal persecution of racial and ethnic minorities.
- Accessory to obstruction of justice for allowing the U.S. vote system to be commandeered by criminals who can rig the vote without being detected.
- Complicity in the assassination of a political rival.

If we had a real attorney general who represented all Americans rather than only the rights of the wealthy, he would investigate these charges, and convene a legitimate investigation into the suspicious atrocities of 9/11/2001. But as he was appointed by the same man who is charged with committing all these crimes, no investigation is likely. In fact, the attorney general himself is probably guilty of many of the same charges as the president, as he is conspicuously involved in so many of the instances of obstruction of justice.

So there is no chance that the sitting government is going to act on these obvious crimes, since the entire government is polluted by conspirators of the same political party who are beholden to the criminals who gave them their jobs. This deadlock also applies to virtually all of the judges in America, since most of them have been appointed by the same manipulators and their like-minded predecessors, who must promise to condone this corruption before they are ever appointed to the bench in the first place.

And even the legislative branch is subject to the same polluting influences, since it costs millions to achieve these posts and once elected, collusion in the secret and criminal activities of the power elite is essential to advancing one's career.

As preposterous as it sounds, the entire Congress (excepting a dozen or so idealists) needs to be dismissed and indicted for its corrupt actions. That says something about the direction our future must take if we are to actually be free.

We are supposed to have a two-party system in America, but it has been apparent for some time that the differences between the two parties are wholly cosmetic. An analysis of the recent vote on making war against Iraq is instructive, as only eight senators opposed it, despite the complete absence of hard evidence that Iraq should be invaded at all (something the rest of the world knows well, but that the American people choose not to know).

The opposition included seven Democrats and one Independent, but the vast majority of Democrats supported the Republican president's position, even though it was clearly a lie. The situation is identical when it comes to the Israelis' continuing theft of the Palestinians' homeland.

Similar outcomes were recorded in the votes for the Patriot Act and Homeland Security bill, two legislative monstrosities which effectively curtailed most of the privileges recorded in our Constitutional Bill of Rights, which had remained essentially unmolested for two centuries.

These votes clearly indicate there is no genuine opposition party in the United States, only a false opposition whose differences with the party in permanent power are cosmetic, not substantive.

This is evident in the opposition party candidates who speak not of changing the current criminal system but only of modifying procedures in trivial ways that would give no relief to the beleaguered citizenry and enrich their corrupt friends instead of the other guy's. Look hard at the principal candidates for the 2004 opposition presidential nomination: a member of the same college fraternity as the current president, and two partisan advocates of immoral support for a foreign power that is a principal abettor of tyranny in the world. This is no opposition, only another flavor of the same oppression. Thus, there is no reason to expect any kind of change after the next election. To put it more clearly, there is no reason to vote at all.

In short, there is no place for the average American citizen to turn for relief. This terminal disease of political corruption extends downward through the states, counties and municipalities, where all elective offices are occupied by people able to pay their way into the ruling system, through alliances with corrupt judges and party bosses, with all machinations based on bribery and deception. Perhaps this is what America has always been—that's a long argument—but there is no argument that this is what America is now: a perverted cesspool of political payola.

Members of both parties were involved in the pivotal decisions of the past half-century that allowed the destruction of America's manufacturing base and the widespread practice of financial deception to cheat legitimate investors out of their hard-earned money. The coming impoverishment of the United States is a bipartisan achievement, but only insofar as the policies of both parties have been consistently to take the short-term profit and feed it quickly to elite investors and their political minions rather than to invest it prudently in the continuing well-being of the American economy.

The flight of industry beyond our borders is chief testament to this policy, and the reason why, when this country goes broke beyond any solution the fast-talkers can fabricate, there will be no fixing the problem, and no ready solution to a chaotic poverty that will sweep the land.

This is the real reason why Ashcroft is talking internment camps, why people are fearful of boxcars with seats in them, and new, barbed-wire enclosures that are supposedly springing up all across the land. The current president is trying to blackmail us into war by insisting the economy needs the boost of a military extravaganza to replenish its treasury with the varied industrial activity that wars always bring. Since World War I, this is a tried-and-true method of reinvigorating the economy. But once we realize the principle means trading millions of foreign lives simply to resuscitate our bank accounts, the true cost of this political principle will surely be our souls.

Judging by America's stances in the world today, this is a price that we—willingly or unconsciously—have already paid. America has lost its soul. Once a beacon of freedom, justice and equality, it is now a blinking neon sign on Skid Row advertising high-interest loans to Third World countries that can never finish repaying them.

We traded our soul when we bribed all those other countries to let us obliterate Afghanistan. There was no real reason to do it, other than to add another layer of deception to the 9/11 caper, to improve political conditions for an oil pipeline, and to put us in better position for when we decide to invade Iran, or Russia, or Saudi Arabia, or Pakistan, or all of the above. There was no real reason to kill all those people except to facilitate additional revenues for military support companies owned by Bush's friends. That's how he's improving our economy, by improving HIS economy and letting a few pennies trickle down here and there.

By allowing this criminal president to get away with his antisocial behavior, the American people don't realize they are only bringing on for themselves what they are now approving for inhabitants of less fortunate countries like Iraq. Sooner or later, the petronazis are going to run out of foreign patsies to bomb, and are going to turn their guns inward. It's inevitable, and to some extent, it has already happened, in terms of the abolition of most of the civil rights we have been accustomed to all our lives.

By acquiescing in the criminal bullying of the rest of the world by the mega-might of the American military machine, we are sending a clear signal to the tyrants in Washington and Tel Aviv that we will tolerate any atrocity as long as our gas prices stay low and our TV schedules are not interrupted. Any day now, you'll begin to notice that the criminal atrocities of the power elite are creeping closer and closer to home.

But don't worry. There'll be TV in the camps, I'm told. But only one channel. And guess who'll be on.

The current system absolutely cannot be fixed. No amount of petitioning, protesting, having meaningful conversations with the few remaining compassionate members of Congress (an endangered species if there ever was one), or writing letters to newspapers that don't care will have any effect. They have no effect now, other than to massage the egos of the deluded activists making the effort.

No, that's too harsh. These are well-meaning people trying to stop an atrocity, but as long as they appeal to forces within the system, these efforts are doomed to failure because they appeal to a fake opposition that has already been co-opted by huge heaps of money.

No outbreak of maverick candidacies, third party movements or political-issue crusades is going to stop this military juggernaut from turning the world into an armed camp (it is already, in case you haven't noticed) where citizens will be herded into "debtors" camps.

Many will be eliminated by vaccination programs, although as the insurance industry collapses, medical care will no longer be available to anyone but the super rich. Already, our schools are assuming the appearance of military indoctrination centers that preach that the poor are evil. Drugs and electronic conditioning will make it easier to turn these elite students against their fellow human beings.

The world is devolving into a universal system of guards and prisoners, and you get to choose which one you will be on the basis of how steadfastly you adhere to the party line. Already, there is nowhere to escape as satellites can access every square inch of the planet, and gun-toting politicians in every single country are ready and willing to turn you in to the thought police because the bounties for such apprehensions are already very lucrative.

This is what will happen if the current system is allowed to remain in place. The alternatives are almost as scary. Whatever happens is going to involve massive dislocation and death, because people in all the industrialized countries are simply not equipped to survive when their support systems break down. People who live in underdeveloped countries are actually better equipped to survive, because they live closer to nature and are less likely to lose their livelihoods in the event of worldwide economic collapse, which, by the way, is imminent.

Yet, breaking down the support systems is exactly what must happen if legitimate freedom is ever to be regained. It is the support systems that enslave us and keep us dependent on our corporate keepers. We need to eat food we grow in our backyards, not buy from supermarket chains.

We need to be able to complain to our government face-to-face, not have to write a letter to Washington, or some other capital that doesn't care. We need to be able to teach our children what we think is important, not what some overpaid consultant in a big city deems is necessary to turn our kids into the next generation of corporate slaves.

We have, over the last century, traded our freedom for that illusory curtain of security that we thought would allow us to live our lives in peace and freedom. Little did we know that this curtain was wholly predicated on the ability and willingness to make war. And now we are beginning to learn that our freedom, all this time, was really a kind of slavery.

Now we find ourselves in a situation that is little better politically than landless serfs were in the Middle Ages at the mercy of their whimsical lords. We have our own lords, and they don't mind killing us and anybody else if we interfere with their moneymaking operations.

If we keep the system, we keep our chains, we keep our right, if we're lucky, to have lucrative jobs as long as we say the right thing, and ignore it when our government decides it must slaughter a large bloc of hapless peasants because they are interfering with access to a valuable natural resource. We can't keep the system and remain free.

The price of either path will be painful.

Assuming you ever get the chance, which will you choose?

In regard to the charges against George W. Bush listed at the top of this chapter:

Military desertion? See http://www.awolbush.com/ or http://www.wearepower.org/pipermail/natlpower/2002-October/000556.html

Cocaine smuggling? See http://www.umsl.edu/~skthoma/offline9.htm

Conspiracy to destroy landmarks and commit mass murder? How about http://emperors-clothes.com/indict/indict-1.htm to pick the best of many stories like this.

Treason: http://bush-treason.blogspot.com/

Accessory to the theft of billions of dollars in the savings and loan debacle: See http://www.thetip.org/art_146_icle.html and http://www.campaignwatch.org/more1.htm

Enriching his friends: http://www.bushnews.com/bushmoney.htm, http://www.bushwatch.net/bushmillions.html and http://www.nrdc.org/bushrecord/other_more.asp

Obstruction of justice: http://members.tripod.com/~RedRobin2/index-93.html

Illegal jailings:
http://www.wsws.org/articles/2002/may2002/pows-m31.shtml and http://newsandevents.utoronto.ca/bin2/thoughts/comment020128.asp

Computerized election vote fraud:
http://www.talion.com/vote-rigging.html

Assassinating a political rival:
http://www.democraticunderground.com/duforum/DCForumID43/5351.html and http://www.wsws.org/articles/2002/oct2002/well-o29.shtml

18

The world can't trust what America says

The key to integrity, this old Mayan guy once told me, is admitting our faults. If we don't do that, our whole lives are built on a bed of lies. This is the United States of America 2003 version—built on a bed of lies and disintegrating all around us.

The situation makes some of us think that the Ayatollah (if you're old enough to remember him—the Iranian religious leader who presided over the taking of American hostages in 1979) was right: America is the Great Satan, he said. But I guess it's not important to Americans anymore to tell the truth. I mean . . . just look at everything.

The greatest military attack on American soil has not even been investigated. Three thousand people killed in downtown New York City and it's just swept under the rug as the insane media manipulators rush on to new fabricated crises to cover up the single greatest crime in American history.

Talk about a big lie. Talk about lack of integrity. And the American people, anesthetized as they are with ill-gotten gains, over-the-counter drugs, bad schools and worse TV, don't even raise a collective eyebrow.

Telling the truth is just not important to them anymore, if it ever was.

In fact, if there's one thing obvious in the world today, it's that America does not tell the truth. It says one thing but always means something else. It promises to spread democracy but all it distributes is oil-money-crazed dictatorship and prison or death without trial for anyone who dares to stand in its way.

Is this the America you learned about in school? Is this the America you hoped to create for your children, where a lie is called the truth and everybody nods like dozing crackheads in front of a slum tenement waiting for their next fix?

• • •

It's hard to say you're proud to be an American when George W. Bush is your president. Embarrassed is more like it. And scared.

Whether it was deserved or not, America used to be regarded as a beacon of freedom and justice for the entire world. That's why so many people came here.

But it's radically different now. America is now a Mafia enforcer fleecing poverty stricken countries for protection money. And if those poor banana republics don't pony up, well, the U.S. has plenty of depleted uranium bombs to drop on their children, or financial nooses to tighten around the necks of their shattered economies.

It's sadly amusing that America claims to be a democracy yet so many of its principal allies around the world are murderous dictatorships, with plenty of corrupt despots to recruit as clients who are all-too-willing to rip off their own people. Look no farther than Central America.

Yes, let's not gild the lily. It is protection money, extorted from poor people by the biggest criminal syndicate of them all, the United States of America. That's what NAFTA and the WTO and all these IMF bailouts are all about. Countries get in economic trouble by importing too many alluring products at too high a price from the United States. Then, because corruption is the rule rather than the exception throughout the world, some soulless leader decides to make a bundle by selling off certain of his country's valuable natural resources, but the money doesn't wind up in the coffers of his own country, it winds up in his own private Swiss bank account, to which he safely flees after he is run out of his own presidential palace by an enraged populace. This has been virtual policy in Mexico throughout the 20th century.

And that's if that country is lucky. If that country is unlucky, the corrupt dictator/president doesn't go to Switzerland but instead hangs around and presides over the IMF "bailout," in which the country's principal assets, especially utilities, are sold at bargain-basement rates to Wall Street plunderers, and the hapless nation is forced to undergo "austerity" measures so the New York banks can harvest their exorbitant interest payments.

Austerity measures like hyperinflation and demolition of all social services guarantee any country which bites on the IMF lure an epidemic of poverty as the middle class is reduced to servitude and thrown out in the streets. This is happening all over South America. Just pick a country (that doesn't have oil). Argentina, Uruguay, Bolivia, Peru. One of the top American plunderers, the Bechtel Corp., came into Bolivia, made a deal with American flunkie dictator Banzer (now dead, thank God), took over the water distribution system, and charged residents (peasant dirt farmers) half their average monthly income for water they previously got for next to nothing. For years, the American press has said nothing about this atrocity. Why? Because we essentially do that to every country. That's where American "prosperity" originates.

And God help your country if it DOES have oil. Then the treatment by America will be much worse.

How much more can we say about Iraq? There is absolutely no scintilla of proof that Saddam was about to make any sudden aggressive moves against anyone. We've been bombing him illegally for a dozen years to make sure he didn't use all those nasty chemical and biological weapons we sold him. Half a million Iraqi children have died because we bombed his water systems and then prevented him from acquiring the materials to fix it. That's something for Americans to be proud of. A classic example of Americans refusing to contemplate the ugly truth.

And as long as we're on the subject, there was no legitimate reason for the first Gulf War, either. Iraq had a valid beef against Kuwait, because American oil companies (yes, Neil Bush was involved) were slant drilling into Iraqi oilfields, which is surely an act of economic warfare. Of course, this was never mentioned by the whorish American press.

Look at the other oil countries. Colombia is under permanent siege (both for drugs and oil). Venezuela is currently being wracked by a would-be *coup* that was blatantly fomented by U.S. business interests.

Indonesia and Saudi Arabia are totally repressive military dictatorships, as are all the Stans near the new Caspian Sea oil fields.

Mexico's in our back pocket though we've recently loaned them some money so we can fleece them again.

Throughout the early months of 2003, virtually all democratic countries in the world witnessed massive demonstrations to urge the United States not to throw its poisoned bombs around the Persian Gulf. These demonstrations were not aimed at the great threat Bush and Powell and Rumsfeld are focused on.

The rest of the world (except the neo-Nazi government of Israel) is not concerned about Saddam Hussein. He is no threat to anyone. Most of the bad weapons he had were provided to him by the United States.

No, the rest of the world—as recent polls show so clearly—believes the United States is the greatest threat to peace in the world. And how do you figure to defend America's reputation with all these blatant lies being told in Washington to justify the mass murder of dark-skinned people who have no army with which to defend themselves?

In point of fact, the disgusting little man who supervised the original Iraq deal was none other than our belligerent defense secretary Donald Rumsfeld, who sold chemical weapons to Saddam back in the '80s, shortly after he bestowed another lethal gift on his own citizens in the form of aspartame, the active ingredient used to sweeten Diet Coke and a zillion other things. Aspartame was never formally approved by the FDA except long after the fact, and has been connected to many different health problems. See http://www.rense.com/general/aspar.htm.

What a fine legacy to leave his family: anthrax and aspartame spread all over the world. I'm sure his family must be very proud. What kind of vicious psychotic could be proud to be an American when contemplating Donald Rumsfeld?

And that's to say nothing of Dick Cheney, our surly vice president, who ignored a court order to turn over documents that would have revealed how he and his energy buddies ripped off the state of California for billions of dollars. At the same time, he's reaping billions in profits as his old company gets the support contracts from every single military deployment.

Why have the American people said nothing about this? Why have no U.S. newspapers blown the lid off this thing?

Look at the false characters Bush has surrounded himself with to assure the destruction of the environment and the impoverishment of the American people: corporate shills Whitman and Venemen to "protect" the environment, an ex-general of the army to conduct "diplomacy" with other countries—that general's son to assure that everything on TV eventually comes only from one station, a glossolalia-speaking psychopath to enforce the laws of the country.

Why aren't millions of Americans besieging their elected representatives, demanding an end to all this criminal behavior? Because it wouldn't do any good. All their elected representatives should be indicted themselves. Anyone who ever received a contribution from Enron or Arthur Andersen is obviously an accessory to the robbery of American consumers. All these people belong in the jail at Guantanamo Bay, indefinitely incarcerated without access to lawyers or family under the very terms of the new Orwellian laws they have created.

But there's another reason why this won't happen. It's because the American people have no integrity . . . as individuals, or as a nation. And in that sense, we have only received what we have deserved.

Congratulations America! Now, the entire world can't believe a single thing we say. This is the world we have created for our children.

Continue to scream as we teeter on the edge of the abyss. Right up until that awful moment we fall in, and become as the rest of the world—cringing in terror from the American war machine.

Just remember one thing: in this new century of pre-scripted news alerts and false terror alarms, whatever America says will not be the truth. This is a conscious choice Americans have made of their own volition—to lie about everything.

19

Random ideas for a new society

I live in Florida but the e-mails I got this week came from Michigan, Arizona, Denmark, the UAE, Texas, British Columbia, Hungary, South Africa, Hawaii, the Bronx, Australia, Delmarva, England, Sweden, Vermont, Arkansas, and Venezuela, to name just a few places. All of these messages said essentially the same thing: we thank you for your writing, but we need to know what to do as the U.S. rushes toward war against the entire world, and our police agencies get more and more aggressive about freely-speaking citizens in our own communities.

Do you know when they will be beating down our doors? some of the messages ask. I'm afraid to say anything in public, write many, because if someone tells the cops what I said, they might come and pick me up. I'm afraid for my children, say a few, about what kind of world they will grow up in.

While I'm honored to receive these questions, I'm as puzzled as the writers about how to deal with this new totalitarian police state threat that is growing like a giant radioactive fungus in the United States and engulfing the entire world. America has told so many lies about Iraq, for instance, that people don't really know how to feel about either Iraq or the U.S., although international polls clearly show that most people consider America to currently be the greatest threat to world peace.

The one thing I know for sure is that the entire American power structure—the president and his appointees, the vast majority of judges and prosecutors and police, the Congress and federal regulators—are all not to be trusted because they have all—and you can quibble with the percentage, but it's disgustingly high—proven themselves to be untrustworthy by their previous lies, or cynical votes in legislatures after receiving bribes that are devious and hard to trace. Imagine, almost all of them voted immunity for a drug company that makes a vaccine that ruins the lives of thousands of children with autism.

This stuff happens everywhere in America, and probably the rest of the world, because utter corruption is always the state of the species.

But the level of it, and the widespread resignation about it, has risen to such proportions that nobody can trust anything any public official says anymore, which has resulted in our current state of depression and mistrust.

Not to mention horror at the grisly fact that America is about to invade a poverty-stricken country with essentially no defenses. And we civilized Americans will use the devil's own arsenal of high tech poisons and devices of explosive torture for no valid reason, other than to steal a dictator's oil.

This is neither the action of a democracy nor a republic, nor the choice of a free and just society. It is the selfish act of a petroleum soaked vampire. American pride has become an unmitigated horror.

The American governmental system has completely broken down. Just think about who is in charge of what. The vice president can continually ignore a court order to reveal how he personally helped his billionaire friends rip off billions of dollars from the people of California. And the president can block an investigation into the greatest tragedy in American history without even uttering any reason at all.

OK, we're all agreed. Things are much worse than we ever thought they'd be.

This radical state of corporate-sponsored human self-destruction, I think, demands radical solutions.

I pose some suggestions here only because people have asked me what should be done. I don't pen them because I think they can be instantly implemented, but I just want you all to think about the possible efficacy of the ideas. On our present path of unchecked growth, we are racing toward species suicide, and we're going to take the rest of the biosphere with us.

We need to change direction. Here are some suggestions.

No absentee landlords. I'm not talking about factories, public facilities, or places of business. I'm talking about domiciles that house families. I'm talking about homes.

Absentee landlords are responsible for all the slums of the world, and most of the environmental problems. If a person lives on the premises he or she owns, chances are excellent they will care for it, nurture it, make it comfortable and secure, because that's where they live. If they don't live there, they don't really care about how nice it is, they only care about the profit from it. This is human usury. It should be abolished, and many of world's most pressing problems would be eliminated just by doing this one thing, just by passing this one law. Home ownership would spread across the planet, friendly neighborhoods would be reestablished, and harmony would replace strife if actual owners of homes were interacting with their neighbors in the best interests of the community. This is clear as glass.

Legalize marijuana now. And combine it with a general amnesty for all drug-related convictions that don't involve murder. Louis Armstrong, Paul McCartney, Bill Clinton and Carl Sagan can't be wrong. They all smoked pot and tried to do good things in their sphere of influence in the world. Study after study has shown that teens who smoke pot are more well-adjusted than teens who don't. Look it up on the Internet. But these studies have been suppressed by the same evil corporate influences that helped make cannabis illegal in the first place.

The biggest benefit would be that it would solve most of the world's drug problems. You wouldn't need Prozac if you were stoned and spreading it around, because you'd have too many friends.

Marijuana was outlawed as a result of efforts by the liquor industry, which correctly foresaw that widespread use of weed would seriously impede their profits, and by Dupont, which also correctly foresaw that hemp fiber is far more beneficial and useful than all these petrosynthetics they invented and reaped fantastic profits from.

The hysteria surrounding this subject has inflicted a three-pronged pox on the entire world.

1. It has deprived humanity of a tremendous biological force for peace in the recreational smoking of it. Everybody knows you don't kill people when you're high on pot like you do when you're smashed on alcohol. Think peace, widespread, jovial, fun-loving peace.
2. The illegalization of weed provides governments with a perfect illicit substance, along with cocaine, heroin and opium, to make huge amounts of money to fund their illegal activities that they can't possibly get approved in a public budget. Think about what Britain did to China. Think about Iran-Contra, where the conservative hero Ronald Reagan and his fascist flunkie Oliver North funneled South American cocaine to dealers in the United States to pay for the weapons they illegally sold to Iran to get them to KEEP our hostages in prison until after Jimmy Carter was defeated in the 1980 election. The current U.S. military activities in Colombia, Kosovo, Afghanistan and to some extent Iraq are about maintaining their satanic hold on the world's drug trade as they are about anything else.
3. Spurious drug convictions account for more than 50% of all current U.S. prison inmates. These are some of the best and brightest people in our society who are actually recruited by paid law enforcement bounty hunters to swell the American prison population in order for prison industries to have more suckers working at 11 cents an hour. Low wages enable those politically connected companies to manufacture office furniture (Internet: Unicor) and other saleable doodads at a

lower cost, and thereby deprive non-convicted Americans of jobs in these industries. American furniture companies can't compete with slave prison labor. Sadly, it is the pill-popping, beer-swilling American cops who put innocent and naïve potheads in jail, who are the real criminals.

Legalize marijuana now and the world will almost instantly become a better place, no question about it.

Unconditional pardon for Leonard Peltier. Of all the atrocities we have committed, the greatest stain on the American soul is the callous extermination of 60 million Native Americans over the 400 year period of our history. And this is a genocide that continues to this day, as the U.S. continues to rob a far more noble race than our own of their basic dignity and security.

If you've read Peter Matthiessen's famous *In the Spirit of Crazy Horse*, you know beyond doubt that Peltier was railroaded into prison without a shred of evidence for the 1974 murders of two FBI agents. Numerous investigations since have only reinforced that popular perception; yet, the forces of the police state continue to maintain their lie while at the same time one of South Dakota's most prominent politicians, Senator Janklow, continues to evade responsibility for the rape and murder of a young Indian girl around the same time Peltier was unjustly convicted.

After 28 years in Leavenworth, Leonard Peltier continues to be the spiritual leader of the oppressed American Indian community.

He is America's Nelson Mandela. A truly humane and conscientious country with the merest whit of honesty would pardon him immediately. He would make a much better president than the one we currently have, certainly.

All Jews must leave Israel. The nation of Israel, which has caused such consternation in the world's oldest neighborhood, is a totally illegal and immoral entity. It was rammed down the throats of the rest of the world by the U.S. and Britain, after a half-century of plotting and bribery. When the vote was taken in the United Nations in 1947, the entire world voted against the idea; yet, Israel was established. Since that time, Zionist terrorists have stolen the land of its original inhabitants, imprisoned them, tortured them, murdered them, and now it wants to deport the rest of them.

All of this has come about because Jews, suffering from centuries of neglect and inbreeding, misread their own holy teachings, and in their pain came to believe that Zion was a geographical location, rather than what it really is: a place in the heart. As a consequence, Jews have misinterpreted what it means to be "the Chosen" people.

Especially given the discrimination they have suffered down through the ages, Jewish contributions in the world have been astonishing in many fields. Our fundamental perceptions of the world have been shaped by Jewish intellectuals like Freud, Einstein and Weinberg. But unfortunately, horrible persecution caused their political perception to become skewed; hence the perceived need for a fortress on earth, rather than the fortress in the heart they already possess.

Realizing this, the time will soon come for Jews to return to their real ethnic homelands in Poland, Ukraine and Argentina, where their creative efforts are sorely needed. They of course would be more than welcome in their satellite homes in South Florida and New York City, which are testaments to the Jewish genius for comfort and fellowship.

Since they have chosen to reject the fallible concept of an afterlife embraced by all of the other major religions on this earth, Jews will come to understand that their true mission as "the Chosen" means that God chose them to make a heaven on earth, and to assist all the peoples of the earth who are less enlightened than themselves in this honorable task.

And as they travel and spread their genius for brotherhood and intellectual achievement, they will remain secure in the knowledge that their Muslim brethren, in accordance with the teachings of Muhammad, will continue to preserve and protect and grant universal access to the Jewish holy sites. This is Allah's will.

A worldwide political and government "stand down" for ethical auditing. If humanity ever succeeds in implementing a truly just and functional society, in about the year 2500 A.D. the history books will speak of an event that happened somewhere along the way when the peoples of the world realized they could achieve better security and a more fulfilling satisfaction by better understanding what their governments actually did and who was actually running things.

Since civilization was first created around 3000 B.C., societies had been centered on military power and economic exploitation, often called by the neutral name "trade." But when the Earth's population reached unsustainable levels, around 2000 A.D., the peoples of the world realized that more planning was necessary to survival, that previous formulas of unending growth were only applicable if the planet's population continued to increase. Economic growth, therefore, became impossible—an injurious objective—when Earth's population growth declined toward a relatively unchanging number.

If we in fact survive as a species, somewhere along the line we will look back and see that we finally realized there were limits to growth.

The realization that growth was an outmoded illusion would have compelled leaders to discuss ways to alter the dominant economic paradigm from one of growth to one of maintaining stability. They realized this data could not be realistically gathered by a small cabal of men who controlled far-flung corporate entities with post-industrial technological magic, but only by actual community leaders who knew firsthand the intimate details of the actual neighborhoods they were involved in.

This epiphany, so long in coming, would have begun an inevitable geopolitical trend toward genuine democratic decentralization, the thousands of representatives of which each contributed personnel to an egalitarian, worldwide police and judicial system that was not dominated by any single powerful entity (as it is now). This system would have necessarily produced far more arguments than the present system, but because of the egalitarian worldwide police and justice systems not dominated by any one power source, would have resulted in far fewer actual conflicts.

Essential to creating the genuinely egalitarian nature of this control system would have been "the stand down," or hiatus of the existing, corrupt political system, to be thoroughly dissected by the world's moral and educational leaders. Representatives of religious disciplines would have been excluded—or at least segregated—from this great conference, because a consensus of leaders and people would have realized that the old American idea of separation of church and state was essential to realistic dialogue, something our current president has worked so hard to destroy.

As Paul Harrison of the World Pantheist Movement has so eloquently pointed out, religion is separate from the earth—there is no real connection between religious precepts and geographical locations on Earth, other than for purposes of outmoded ritual—hence, there is no real point to including religious protocols to matters that involve geography and economics, other than a general prayer that these discussions would be conducted honestly and for the benefit of all.

Now, lapsing back out of the science fiction mode to the present political impasse on this planet, I see no hope of restoring the integrity of the United States without this kind of government "stand down," or hiatus, where all federal officers and judges are genuinely investigated by a politically impartial FBI for improper business dealings and criminal activity. I am supremely confident that the vast majority of officeholders in America in the year 2003 would wind up in jail as a result of this investigation. (Are you listening, Bill Frist?)

I understand that this essay is all utopian fantasy. This is a world where we talk about justice but don't really mean it. All the political badinage about helping this segment of society or that poor country is all just doubletalk as cynical aristocrats jockey for position to improve their public image at the expense of millions of anonymous poor people.

These ideas may be fantasy—especially the interrogation of corrupt governments, based on an imaginary viewpoint from the far future that we actually succeeded in creating a civilization to be proud of.

In point of fact, our civilization is something we cannot be proud of. Insincerity and duplicity rule. What appears in our public print little reflects the criminal machinations of a power elite that exploits the poor in every nation. Our most sincere teachers propagate myths that lead our children toward hate and discrimination, and our leaders mumble deliberately false propaganda that leads our impressionable offspring to believe that America is a land of truth and justice. The most percipient of the older generation eventually come to realize that the basic dynamics of civilization have not really changed in 5000 years, and that the truth is bought and distributed by rich men to minds that have been deliberately shaped to not understand what is actually going on.

In lapsing back from future science fiction to contemporary political reality, I am forced to admit that it would be my fondest wish to see the entire U.S. Congress, all members of the presidential administration, all justices and judges above the level of normal courts arrested and jailed without trial and without access to lawyers for the encyclopedia of crimes they have all committed.

I would like to see President Bush, Vice President Cheney, his entire Cabinet and the Department heads Bush has named, shipped to and incarcerated at Guantanamo without access to counsel under penalties for aiding terrorists that they themselves created in the Patriot Act.

But I know this won't happen. I know the world is not a noble place where justice does not rule—only money does. And this is why we continue, hellbent and headfirst, on our path to the destruction of own species and most of the other ones, too.

20

The real terrorist is George W. Bush

America is frightening the world. The vaunted beacon of freedom has turned into a Ku Klux Klan bonfire.

Maybe some sadists think that's a good idea, but the genuinely decent people of this planet surely don't.

Incited by an endless barrage of dubious bluster about the sudden need for all-out war against a bomb-ravaged Third World nation, people in 38 different countries came out by the hundreds of thousands on February 15, 2003 to sound the alarm about this spreading American madness.

And we all know the reason why.

The man who claims to lead the fight against terror is terrorizing the entire world.

He terrrorizes little old American ladies by making them strip naked at airports and having their private parts probed by minimum-wage security Nazis searching for weapons of mass destruction. He terrorizes allies around the world with bribes and threats into saying exactly what he says regardless of what they actually think. He terrorizes opposition party politicians into nervous silence when planes fall out of the sky with no explanation.

The belligerent little twit from Texas singlehandedly has turned the world's greatest democracy into a paranoid police state. He recently killed 5,000 people in Afghanistan without a shred of verifiable evidence, and now is threatening to do it again . . . and again and again and again.

No single person in recent history has motivated so many people in so many places to interrupt their daily lives and stand out on some strange street in order to try to save the lives of innocent people they've never met.

Colossal demonstrations took place in cities all over the United States, from Portland to Tampa to Montpelier. Washington drew 500,000 and San Francisco saw 200,000 (although the pro-war, corporate shill TV networks cynically refuse to confirm those totals). Concerned people protested all over Europe as well, from London to Istanbul, and in Brazil, Japan and New Zealand. There was even a peace demonstration in Antarctica.

Yet the plans for another United States war against its former ally Iraq continue at a frenzied pace, with rumors circulating across the Internet that America will begin dropping bombs on the Iraqi people at the exact moment George W. Bush delivers his State of the Union address.

How cynically telegenic! Death from the sky as a hot new TV show.

Despite all the hysterical mumbo jumbo about unending terror alerts that never seem to materialize and draconian new laws that have gutted America's fabled Bill of Rights, people of the world with the intelligence to analyze events without the aid of cutesy but ignorant commentators on the Fascist News Network (a.k.a. Fox) know that all the pro-war propaganda is just a screen of strident lies.

People know America wants to steal Iraq's oil, and if the U.S. gets away with this, there will be no reason for it not to continue its Genghis Khan-like rampage into Iran and Saudi Arabia, all the while trumpeting the hollow mantras of "national security" and "war on terror."

This is exactly the rationale a falsely speaking America used in Vietnam. "We had to destroy the village in order to save it." Only now it's: "In order to fight terror we must use terror." It's all just another variant of Orwell's "war is peace."

America wants to enslave the entire world to make it "free."

Another *raison d'etre* for this continuing American aggression in Iraq is Israel, which seeks to expand its own borders far beyond what they are now. Palestinian exiles would fit nicely into the plans of this conscienceless neo-Nazi state.

I myself, however, don't believe that either oil or Israel are the primary reasons behind this new Iraq attack. I believe it's really about controlling the focus of the news, manipulating the opinions of the population, and most of all, deflecting attention from the hunt for who really engineered the World Trade Center disaster.

And, to a lesser extent, to divert the public's attention from the criminal activities of Enron, Halliburton, and Harken, which robbed and in some cases continue to rob the American people of billions of dollars at the exact time when the American stock exchange is essentially bankrupt and certainly unworthy of the attention of intelligent investors.

A war in Iraq keeps people from focusing on these more important issues, and the petro-connected corporate news media are only too willing to assist Bush in the deception.

Just look at what has happened in the recent past. When people began asking questions about the 9/11 horror, anthrax attacks were invented to deflect the public's attention.

When crucial votes about new security measures effectively nullifying the U.S. Constitution caught the public's eye, terror alert after terror alert grabbed the headlines, and the USA Patriot Act was passed without most of the members of Congress even reading it.

Then, when the Enron effluent finally hit the fan, after tens of thousands of people had been robbed of substantial amounts of money by Texas billionaires, suddenly Iraq became a pressing problem, and the mass media has scarcely looked elsewhere since. It has had absolutely no time or space to properly investigate Vice President Cheney's conspiracy with energy executives to fleece the populace in the biggest scam since the S&L fire sales, which not-so-coincidentally was another Bush operation.

Now, I'm sitting here on this bright, chilly Saturday morning watching CNN blab on about the supposed pros and cons of getting the government-mandated smallpox vaccine, but of course the beautiful anchor people fail to mention the most salient fact about this issue: that all smallpox epidemics throughout history have been caused by vaccination programs. This program was invented as a response to those staged anthrax attacks, which have never been solved and were dropped from the media lineup when the trail seemed to lead right back to the government.

When was the last time you heard a word about the criminal activities of Enron, or all those other corporations which helped enrich our leaders while it screwed ordinary people?

But most important, when was the last time you heard a whisper about why the U.S. air defenses ALLOWED the 9/11 attacks to happen, why fires at the bases of three towers burned for 100 days, or why billions of dollars changed hands in stock machinations in the days immediately preceding this unprecedented tragedy?

A long time, for sure. All we've heard for the last six months is how Saddam is connected to al-Qaeda (not proven), how Iraq is hiding weapons of mass destruction (not proven), and how Iraq is an imminent threat to the security of the United States (you couldn't prove this in a court of law even if you bought the whole jury!). And all these repetitive lies have served the purpose of the criminals in charge, to distract us from the truly important issues.

That's why Bush can calmly comment about how peace demonstrations are a natural and expected part of American "freedom." Although these statements make many people vomit for their blatant insincerity, he can express this thought because the demonstrations are an unwitting part of the coverup of the more important questions, which certainly are about what cabal of insiders engineered the execution of this "new Pearl Harbor" that a Republican think tank so urgently recommended more than a year before the 9/11 tragedy.

Whatever happened to Osama bin Laden? He disappeared faster than last year's hot new sitcom. I believe—if he is not dead, or never existed in the first place—that someone in American intelligence knows exactly where Osama bin Laden is, but that he's fulfilled his contract with the CIA, served his purpose, and now is to be left alone. Hell, he's probably in the federal witness protection program.

And what of al-Qaeda, the mystery revolutionary group that these days is blamed for just about every untoward event in the entire world?

Al-Qaeda, like Saddam Hussein and Manuel Noriega, was originally funded by the United States for geopolitical intrigues in Central Asia. This relationship, like the one with bin Laden, supposedly ended somewhere along the way, but the people who are telling us this are the same big media buffoons who insists that smallpox shots are safe, that Iraq is an imminent threat to the security of the United States, and that polls say Bush is the cat's meow.

Maybe he's the dead cat's meow.

I don't know if it's really fair to call George W. Bush a terrorist president, because he is really only using the terrroristic threat of using the American military to get what he wants politically. But on the other hand, as in signing all those Texas executions, he does seem to be enjoying it; a Napoleonic martinet strutting upon the stage with his draft-dodging cronies, playing commander-in-chief with a war chest of deadly, high-tech toys. So maybe it is fair to call him a terrorist president.

There's an old biker legend that insists: when you fire a bullet at someone in anger, that bullet will—someday, someplace, someway—come back on you.

Or, to put it more simply, as you sow, so shall you reap. Just think about what's coming to us as a result of how our unelected president has terrorized the whole world.

The real terrorist is George W. Bush.

21

A rabid flock of lying killers

How American Christians and Jews justify the mass murder of innocents in the name of "The Lord"

Does God want us to kill innocent Iraqi children? Judging by the apparently unanimous approval in the Senate chamber from all those truth-immune political celebrities watching President Bush's most recent State of the Union address—all of whom are at least overtly religious churchgoers—the message is clear: HE does.

Apparently there is not a single member of Congress who opposes the idea of dropping more bombs on Iraq. Sure, there are a few who want U.N. endorsement, but if they get that—that is to say, if they can ultimately avoid blame for this atrocity by later saying the U.N. said it was OK to do it—there is nobody in the entire U.S. government apparatus who opposes obliterating Iraq, and murdering still thousands more of its defenseless women and children.

If there were, we would have heard them booing that speech, and we didn't.

If there were, we would have heard an outraged Democratic response, instead of the cowardly endorsement of the principles of the Bush plan for continuing genocide that we did hear.

Imagine—not a single member of Congress who will stand up for the most important teaching of Jesus, for the idea that killing large numbers of innocent people for some nebulous and unprovable political assertion is wrong—not only wrong but evil and contemptible. Not only nebulous and unprovable, but deliberately deceitful, because it is not Iraq that has weapons of mass destruction, but Israel—and Americans have no objection to that, even though Israel has unjustly murdered a thousandfold more innocent victims than Iraq has over the past decade.

We don't want freedom for the Iraqis; we just want their oil, and the whole world knows this.

The shadow of death is the heart of darkness emanating from the teachings of Jesus Christ and his bloodthirsty father Yahweh, according to these sanctimonious posers in Washington who describe themselves as born-again Christians and devout Jews.

It is now clear that the real axis of evil runs right through the heart of Washington, D.C., and—judging by the polls—right through the hearts of the American people.

For it is the most righteous churchgoers—the followers of Bible-thumping, Armageddon-preaching, Moonie-funded televangelists—who are at the rabid forefront of this call for unjust mass murder, as they nod their heads in agreement and applaud the obviously false statements of George W. Bush preaching massacre and mayhem against all the dark-skinned peoples of the world as his latest "faith-based" initiative. Obedience to a corrupt church is easily twisted into obedience to a corrupt government.

Yet while the evangelical fundamentalists lead the charge toward their desired Armageddon, it is the level-headed respectable Episcopalians and Methodists and Jewish liberals who by their criminal silence provide the real ballast in the immoral inaction of the status quo, by their failure to condemn the bloodthirsty hysteria of their less-temperate brethren.

They bow their heads and feign sublime theological conviction as they utter their devout prayers that their leaders fry the innocent children of foreign countries with radioactive weaponry devised in the deepest bowels of hell.

And for this sincere wish, they contemplate their own reward of a peaceful afterlife in a righteous heaven. None for me, thanks. Can you imagine hanging out with these freaks for eternity?

• • •

I had an argument a long time ago with someone very close to me. It was that classic "follow the words of God's holy law vs. doing good works" debate.

I contended that it really didn't matter what religion you practiced, or if you practiced one at all. As long as you lived an honest life, tried to help the downtrodden, were kind to the less fortunate, and took the stand of rightness against opinions you deemed to be unjust, then you were more likely to be regarded with favor in the eyes of God than you would be if you just went to church on Sunday and screwed people the rest of the week.

Being a devout and vociferous Christian, she vehemently disagreed with my assessment. She said, basically, that it didn't matter what kind of good works one did, but rather, that as long as people failed to sincerely accept Jesus Christ as their Lord and Savior, and followed verbatim the words that were written in the Holy Bible, they were going straight to hell, and that was the end of it.

If you'd just read the book of Revelation, she said condescendingly, you'd know the rules of the game. We win in the end. That's all there is to it.

And that was essentially the end of the argument. There was no bridging the gap.

At the time, I perceived her inflexible protestations as the very definition of madness.

Many years later, I now contend this is the very argument that keeps the world ever on the brink of war. Encouraged by their church, ever eager to improve its influence on the powers that be, people who insist "holy" laws must be followed to the letter and not challenged, extend that self-centered self-righteousness to their political leaders. The feigning faithful fervently declare that the judgments of their leaders must not be questioned. These leaders must have our best interests at heart, they reason, because they are our leaders. This is why politicians rush to embrace religious factions. This kind of voter loyalty is not something you could get from a sane person.

By this method, I believe that piety leads to tyranny, that wholehearted devotion to creed results in a kind of kneejerk fascism that prevents critical scrutiny of decisions by parable-parroting politicos who just might, when they make political pronouncements, possibly have motives that are less than sincere.

Those who believe in the infallibility of Scripture are a lot less likely to perceive these dishonest motives, because they have been taught to believe, rather than to think. They have been taught to blindly hope, rather than percipiently perceive.

So when these leaders murmur familiar phrases about Christian values and ideals, and their voters choose to believe them, the people extend this same blanket allegiance to politicians that they voluntarily give to their chosen church. And because so much of their own delusional self-image is tied up in this allegiance, they are unable or unwilling to perceive faults in these leaders that are blatantly obvious to others who are not shackled by the profound handicap of blind faith.

These are the shackles of religious belief. This is the prison of God, which now threatens to destroy the planet.

Worse, these same pious politicians deliberately pander to these poor folk who believe rather than think, further ingratiating themselves in the minds of people who are desperate to believe the best and pretend the worst does not exist, especially in their own midst.

I believe that these are the people who are really responsible for the callous and needless murders the United States government commits every day, all around the world. I believe it is the people who dress up every Sunday morning and tuck their bibles under their arms, smile at their neighbors and partake of Christian fellowship who are ultimately responsible for the cynical high-tech butchery that continues to ravage the innocent population of Iraq, and so many other defenseless Third World countries.

They profess that their faith in God is unshakeable even as they see with their own eyes that the leaders they put their trust in are murdering innocent people in the name of the very God they worship devoutly.

Americans (and Europeans before them) have a penchant for killing and then inventing some kind of excuse to justify it as God's work.

Devout so-called Christian authorities tortured and murdered countless millions of "heathens" because the victims refused to accept Jesus Christ. Or, the perpetrators refused to believe people who said they did accept the prescribed messiah. Or, worst of all, as in the case with Columbus and the Spanish conquistadors, people were killed because they couldn't speak the required language, and this was taken as a sign of disbelief.

Of course, Christians are not alone. The Jewish people are currently engaged in a pogrom of their own that matches the most horrid behavior of any people in history as they gun down babies and old women in their quest to complete the theft of land from its underprivileged and persecuted Arab inhabitants. Muslims have their own religious horrors to be ashamed of as well: the beheading of minor miscreants for misdemeanors, and demanding women live their lives in shrouds because men can't control their own penile fantasies.

But persecution of women is what religions of that type are all about, and it exists in spades in all three creeds. Remember that Jewish prayer: thank God I was not born a woman. Or the Christian ban on birth control to keep women from ever attaining equal status with men. And those Muslim burkas.

It is religious conviction that keeps us from seeing the truth, the priests and rabbis and mullahs who preach hatred of the stranger, and the deep-seated fear of ordinary people who are afraid to speak the truth for fear of persecution that grips the entire world.

Perhaps the last group is the worst offender against the religious precepts they insist they espouse. Because this fearful silence allows hypocritical killers to ply their trades, the really guilty party in the continuing U.S. war against the entire world are ordinary churchgoers whom you see every Sunday dressed in their finery. It is their cowardly silence and unquestioning obedience to authority that ultimately allows these horrors to continue. It is the silence of ordinary Americans too busy with their trivial pursuits or too cowed by their striving for illusory status that is ultimately to blame for the needless extermination of so many fine and innocent souls all over the world.

As a disaffected ex-CIA agent now living in another country once told me, "Americans are not a very nice bunch of people."

• • •

Now, at this juncture, many of you have no doubt noticed my failure to be as vehement in my contempt for Muslims and Hindus and other sects as I have been for hypocritical Christians and Jews. Therefore, I must be spreading Muslim or Hindu propaganda as my way of undermining the principles of moral, God-centered America. Let me assure you it is only because I have lived my whole life in America, and have met insufficient numbers of Muslims and Hindus to be able to comment on their practices as directly as I can about Christians and Jews.

Having said that, I can also say that the paradigmatic parable of the insanity of all religions that I use most often derives from the Hindu epic, *Bhagavad-Gita*, in which Lord Krishna advises Prince Arjuna that it doesn't really matter how many people are killed in battle because all souls eventually come to him anyway; so go ahead and begin the slaughter.

And although I have recently heard an evocative passage from the teachings of Mohammed about his prescription for tolerance and care of the shrines of other religions, I certainly can be no fan of a philosophy that prescribes death to women for flirting, a practice the Taliban recently favored.

Nevertheless, it is obvious to me—and precious few others—that the events of 9/11 were a ruse principally designed to defame the Muslims of the world, to provide an excuse for their persecution and a justification for the invasion of the Middle East oilfields by Western corporations. Every political event of the 20th cenury—and in some respects long before that—has masked a subtext involving the collective enslavement and defamation of all people in that part of the world, and all these events since the Crusades have been generated by Christian and/or Jewish colonial interests. Just look at the histories of all the Middle Eastern countries, which were all (except Iran) initially constructed out of thin air for political convenience by British Petroleum and its allies.

Just look deeply into the creation of al-Qaeda, Osama bin Laden, Hamas, Islamic Jihad, Saddam Hussein, the Saudi princes and presidents of Egypt and Pakistan and see how the tentacles of their histories always slither back to 1600 Pennsylvania Avenue.

As is the case now in the American aggression against Iraq, religious propaganda always serves as the convenient cover story for naked political motives, a righteous rhetoric by which to cloak hideous crimes.

We can continue to blame our leaders for their duplicity, but the real fault lies in the hearts of ordinary, God-fearing people. Because they refused to ask the hard questions about the inconsistency of their own beliefs, and particularly in the xenophobic vilification of strangers, they are now unable to bring themselves to ask the same hard questions of their leaders. As a result, much of the world—including themselves—is now dying for no good reason.

If there is any group against whom a preemptive strike is needed in this world, it is those who cower inside chapels of worship and conclude that the power of their chosen belief exempts them from the need to think clearly and feel sincerely about all those people who are being killed in their names.

22

Fake terror alerts

We're as stupid as they think we are

How stupid do they think we are? Only hours after our much-praised Secretary of State is revealed to have been using material plagiarized from a college student to justify why we're going to kill thousands of people with bombs, our government issues a terror alert and expects us to believe it?

And how stupid are we? We believe it.

Everybody takes it seriously even though Colin Powell has been shown to have perpetrated a colossal lie before the entire world, sitting in front of the assembled multitude of rectitude at the United Nations, exposed as having tried to pass off a post-graduate thesis about conditions a decade ago as supposedly cutting-edge Department of Defense intelligence. Used before the most august leaders of the world, this is supposed to be the best we can do? For all that money in the defense budget?

I mean, shouldn't we be embarrassed to be caught in such a childish lie? Could the U.S. government have reached a new low in their sluggish and unintelligent efforts to convince the world it should bomb everything that doesn't "love our freedom?"

But it didn't matter. The American people have become such dullards that apparently nobody made the connection concerning lying about the reasons for bombing Iraq and lying about the terror alert. Certainly not the TV news robots.

Stupidest of all? The terror alert was meant to cover up the Secretary of State's very own sophomoric *faux pas*, but the piggies needn't have bothered.

The TV anchorpeople, who worry a lot more about their hair than they do the fate of the world, didn't even blink an eye, didn't even make the connection, that if Powell is fabricating evidence culled from the out-of-date research—the grad student's work was assessing conditions in Iraq long ago—then what possible evidence could this most "humane" member of the Bush Cabal of Death have been using to suddenly whip up a new terror alert—which served no greater purpose than to take the world's focus off his own obvious incompetence and insincerity.

His own lies. There could be no clearer evidence that the United States is lying—not only about its own objectives but also about its own methods, its own performance—and, as I'm sure our genuine enemies would notice, and most dangerous of all—its actual capabilities. There may be no doubt that the U.S. could totally vaporize Baghdad, and no doubt that America's demonic weapons of mass destruction have turned large swaths of Third World countries into radioactive wastelands, but there are real doubts that this two-faced gang of armchair cutthroats have the ability, the will or the intent to defend our country.

Just look at the investigation into 9/11, the biggest crime in American history, and let me know if you see one. Just look at Enron, the biggest robbery in American history, and let me know if you see the big perps being brought to justice.

Lies. Everywhere you turn are lies, couched in trite buzz-phrases, uttered by incompetent functionaries like Ashcroft, who couldn't even make a decent middle school debate team, not to mention Bush, who will never learn that sincere statements later learned to be false mean you can never reach people again.

Or maybe you can. Maybe people don't really care if the world is destroyed, if their own sons return to the Fatherland contaminated by radioactivity and poison vaccines. The insincerely enraptured media suckups, who have their own challenges to overcome, insist

Bush is popular, but average people at the shopping center now only say that if they think the Homeland Security camera is on them.

Lies. Like the new information about the Patriot missiles that the U.S. has sold to practically every country that wanted one. During the first Gulf War massacre, the Pentagon claimed a 100 percent kill-ratio against those evil Scud missiles launched by Saddam. Now the news is the Patriot missiles never hit a single Scud, or that the kill-ratio was somewhere in the range of 7 percent, at best.

Just like the phony U.S. missile tests we see in the news every now and then. Those missiles can't hit spit unless there's a GPS beacon in the target. But the well-coiffed media harlots always report those tests as if they were some actual triumph of technology, rather than the totally bogus corporate political propaganda they are. Speaking of that, did you hear Raytheon, the company that made the Patriot missiles, was also hired to evaluate their performance, for a cool half million? It's the Arthur Andersen principle, still working fine.

Our genuine enemies—as opposed to the ones cooked up at CIA secret meetings and funded covertly by third parties (are you listening, Bob Graham?)—must be noticing that a Patriot missile couldn't hit a mule in the ass with a banjo.

Just like the phony scripted news alerts on CNN that don't mean anything, either—they just condition people to ignore all news alerts—all this talk about terror alerts reveals to our genuine enemies that we are all bluster without competence, all talk and no game, not to mention genuine toughness. Living the soft life of the complacent West, we rely on our high-tech toys to do our killing for us, and when those toys don't work, those softie Western soldiers have a real problem, like crashing their own helicopters or bombing their own allies because they're doing too many drugs. Too bad the war on drugs doesn't work on the drugs used for war.

The only reason for this terror alert was to take the focus off Powell's laziness, his unprofessional reliance on a British report that was nothing more than verbatim excerpts from an out-of-date war college paper, which he passed off as the best the American government could produce about its knowledge of what is really going on in Iraq. An utterly pathetic and incompetent performance by a government that has received a permanent free pass from uncritical media stooges.

These stooges are fakes themselves, and so is Powell, and so are his terror alerts. And by their belief in all these false statements—these fake terror alerts—so are the American people, who have become, in the eyes of so many innocents abroad, the scourge of the earth, for their misinformed malice and imbecilic indifference.

The biggest terror alert of all—9/11—was an event manufactured by the very people who are supposed to be our leaders, our benefactors, not our plunderers. Don't argue—the evidence is plentiful, despite the stalled official investigation. Now, the biggest worry becomes the matter of when they will decide we need another dose to convince us we are in danger and they are our saviors.

9/11 occurred at a time when the cabal was devising new and draconian restrictions on our freedom called the Patriot Act, which was passed shortly after that disaster. Now comes word that a new Patriot Act II has been devised in secret, intensifying the insulting horrors created by the first one.

Can we make the connection between the act of writing the new rules for totalitarian control and the horrendous act necessary to justify its imposition? And can we make it in time?

Not likely, because we're as stupid as they think we are.

23

America's autopsy report

As American civilization limps into the year 2003, one thing is certain: there is no reason for any person who aspires to any degree of intelligence or authenticity to be reading a daily mainstream newspaper or watching network television news. All they do is distract your attention from where it should be focused.

Page after page, show after show, scripted news "alerts"—written at political party headquarters, approved by corporate moneymen, spewed forth by pretty robots fresh out of modeling school—dominate the monologues.

War is a TV show. Honest journalism—like Republican functionary Dick Armey said about the Constitution—is an outmoded and dysfunctional concept, because it doesn't directly apply to increasing profitability.

Those great American products—demeaning of foreigners, pandering to irrational fear, appealing to selfishness and greed—ooze out in story after story, and most important, obscure the real facts that should be the focus of badly needed investigative reports, like industrial pollution condoned by the courts and approved by pseudo-regulators.

Consider current stories about Venezuela, just as a random place to start. U.S. media harp on the failure of its leader, the democratically elected and champion of the poor Hugo Chavez, and insist Venezuelan society is in revolt against a dictator, when the true facts are that U.S. media and a tiny percentage of white Venezuelan businessmen have ordered their employees to sabotage a legitimate democracy, because their corrupt, ill-gotten gains are threatened by someone who only wants justice for all his people, not just the privileged few. It is perhaps the most visible example of how America has tried to bribe people to accept corporate dictatorship while calling it democracy. America continues to do that in virtually every country in the world. As a result, the people in the rest of the world know America is no longer a free democracy, but the people inside the U.S. do not.

Are you, dear reader, the kind of person who wants to hang out with somebody who buys their friends? If you're an American who is not feverishly questioning what the U.S. is doing in the world today, then you ARE one of these losers.

Of course, the Bush vaudeville act about Iraq is the primary example nowadays of this demonic deception. For six months the Bush administration has been inventing reason after reason about why Iraq is a threat to the United States (preposterous on its face) and with each new statement, the world laughs harder and more angrily. Lie after lie, fiction after fiction. Check out the logos on the TV networks: War IS a TV show.

There was no reason to invade Iraq the first time, and there is far less reason today. Most people who read the web carefully know Iraq did not gas the Kurds. The people who read the big newspapers or watch TV don't. They didn't hear about Goldstein's phony story, repeated breathlessly by Brokaw, Blitzer and the rest.

It is just like the lies they told about the World Trade Center, for which they could produce no evidence. Just like the lies they told about Afghanistan: again no evidence. Just a lot of needlessly dead bodies, charges of American torture and mass murder of innocents.

We don't read about this in the newspapers, or hear about this on TV. Only the new strategies against nuclear "threats," Iraq and now North Korea.

Speculations about potential Armageddons, terror attacks on our country that really exist only in the minds of megalomaniacal corporate titans and their emasculated media minions. Not the real news.

The real news is mostly domestic, especially since there is solid evidence of American participation in the creation, execution and cover-up of the World Trade Center and Pentagon tragedies. These are things that will not be discussed in the official investigation (now chaired, incidentally, by someone with business ties to the bin Ladin family, just like Bush is tied—thank you, Global Research).

The real news is how Bush, Cheney, Rumsfeld and their perverted "patriot" friends are stealing the American people blind, primarily through government contracts with companies that either they or their friends own. Check out the Carlyle Group's recent acquisitions. Now they can not only make the vaccines they'll give us, they can also ship their drugs worldwide with a minimum of hassle.

All the stories about Iraq and North Korea have been created to distract attention from that. And if you're reading the newspapers or watching TV, that's all you'll get. Not the real news.

So what news should we really be getting? Here's the short list:

1. **Political corruption.** Virtually the entire Congress should be in jail, just based on the contributions they've accepted from criminal corporations. Dick Armey (him again) took millions from Eli Lilly and winds up inserting lawsuit protection into the Homeland Security bill for the company against its poisonous vaccines, which have condemned thousands of American children to a life of autism. And the whole Congress votes wholeheartedly for this bill. Dr. Bill Frist has just been named Senate Majority leader, and he's one of biggest medical criminals the nation has ever seen, as owner of the humongous HCA hospital corporation, which is renowned for its Medicaid billing fraud and kickbacks to pharmaceutical giants foisting off unsafe drugs on patients. Not to even mention all the crimes committed by Bush—how about thousands of counts of obstruction of justice for starters?—and his Enron-connected appointees.
2. **Responsibility for 9/11.** It's not just about deliberately flubbed air defenses or the calculated ineptitude of military intelligence.

These events were planned at home, using multiple agencies of our government and others, with seriously high-ranking officials like Gen. Myers and Sen. Graham being turned against their own country to support the conspiracy. The leaders of our Congress, both Democrat and Republican, are now the leaders of the cover-up, dutifully nodding at the self-serving pronouncements of talking heads expressly hired to repeat the official line that blames the whole thing on Muslims. Gee, who would want to blame Muslims? Gee, who owns the TV stations?

3. **Dangerous food and drugs.** The phony vaccine scares are just the tip of the iceberg. The anthrax investigation has been completely covered up because the trail led straight to the government's door. There is virtually no food inspection in the entire nation. Fish from farms are full of mercury. Wildlife are dying from mystery diseases and they infect domesticated meat products. The anti-depressant epidemic leads to more suicides and anti-social behavior, and more important, creates zombie citizens who have no interest in political events, as long as they can keep smiling or breathing deeply. Cheney's old company profits from all these war deployments because it provides chow to the troops. Reportedly, the food really sucks. It could do in some of the troops, too, if the depleted uranium ammunition or the poison vaccines don't get them first.

So, this gives you some idea of the magnitude of the disease. The prognosis is terminal. There can be no recovery of a system that is infected with this much criminal activity. There is no fixing this, especially by voting, which has degenerated into widespread electronic fraud. The last election should be totally voided because there is no way to realistically audit the results, especially since criminal fat cats own the voting machines that tabulate the totals any way the owners want.

What will happen is what is happening now. The nation is collapsing into a criminal police state, where the only thing that counts is how much the payoff is. No matter how noble or honest individual sheriffs or legislators are; they're going nowhere against the massive web of corruption now strangling the life out of our once sincere republic.

The Constitution is gone and America is dead. Most people haven't noticed because they're spiritually and intellectually dead themselves. Too much TV and bad schools. Too many life lessons that taught it was not profitable to be honest.

You won't read about this in the newspapers, or hear it on TV. Honest analyses of what's really going are bad for business, not conducive to the marketing of all these unneeded and deceptive products.

In conducting America's autopsy report, there was a fundamental rule to be followed: If it was good for business it was bad for people. This is why the disease of greed was fatal. Our leaders stopped telling the truth a long time ago, and when the time came when telling the truth became essential to our survival, they just couldn't remember how.

Because they were paid not to.

24

The 'Dead Zone' scenario

These days hang heavy, languid, dreamlike. I imagine how it must have been sitting in a park on the coast of France staring at the gray ocean sky in those dreary days right before World War II. The Nazis had stolen your country and you wondered how long it would be before your life, if you kept it, would be changed forever. That's about like how it is now as we sleepwalk through these hollow days of well-worn lies, listening intently for the echo of each footstep, as we wait for the bombs to start falling.

It is a common theme used in several short stories I have read, although the only one I can readily identify with was by Ray Bradbury: what would you do if you could go back in time, before the conflagration started, knowing now all the heartache and carnage Hitler had triggered? What would you do? The heroes in some of these fanciful stories—maybe this was a Twilight Zone episode; I'm envisioning the actor Russell Johnson—went back in time and tried to stop the Führer's ruthless rampage before it started.

But the message in all these stories was mostly the same: history could not be changed, and proceeded as the history books surely tell us, despite the best-intentioned efforts of the inspired hero.

More recently, Stephen King's *The Dead Zone* was developed along these lines. In the movie version, it was the eerie Christopher Walken playing clairvoyant Johnny Smith who could read the future and foretell that evil Senate candidate Gregg Stillson, portrayed by Martin Sheen in a masterfully dastardly way, would nuke the world if allowed to achieve his destiny.

Old Johnny, mimicking all those other heroes, decided he had to follow his intuition and save the world from a holocaust, so he went after the demented politician with a thirty-ought-six. He didn't have to kill him, though; the threat was enough to reveal the villain's true character (he tried to hide behind a baby, and all the newspapers snapped the photo). It cost Johnny his life, but it saved the world from disaster.

Oh, if real life only were as simple as popular fiction.

Lately, this archetypal fable has been floating at the periphery of my thoughts. Much in the same way George W. Bush fantasizes about how simple life would be without Saddam Hussein, many others, I'm sure, are having the same thoughts about Bush himself. And not a few of them, I'm equally sure, would put him in the same class of human being with Hitler, since many of his recent achievements bear a striking resemblance to the resumé the Führer so cravenly assembled.

A number of folks lately have suggested such that doing such a number on Bush would be an appropriate remedy for many of the ills of the world, especially in light of recent provisions of the Patriot Act, which mandate instant termination for anybody deemed to be consorting with known terrorists—something our character-challenged commander-in-chief has certainly done simply by hanging out with people like Rumsfeld, a known terrorist if there ever was one. Hey, he sold Iraq its weapons of mass destruction, didn't he?

This radical and illegal recommendation of offing the big boss has lately become known as "pulling a vox," after the suggestion of the popular New York columnist and Internet legend who recommended invoking the Patsy Act provision on Duhbyah. But all that earned the voxman was a midnight visit from forty or so federal agents and the destruction of his website—which lives on, by the way, in numerous and anonymous mirror websites lovingly maintained by admirers who seriously appreciated his suggestion, and his outspoken insistence that the tragic atrocities of Sept. 11, 2001 were an inside job, engineered by the petronazis in Washington, D.C.

These are the stark facts. Current American leaders are proven liars, particularly in the recent cases with Colin Powell at the U.N. and the subsequent terror alert based on the lie of a prisoner. In a court of law, one lie disqualifies all previous and subsequent testimony of any witness. It is not improper to infer that the lies told by the Bush administration in these two instances render everything its lackeys have said as fabrications to hide some other purpose, some other action.

This inference can logically be taken back to the events of 9/11, whose cover-up without investigation has lasted so long that there can be no doubt that the official version of those events—blaming Osama bin Laden and saying the American defense apparatus was taken by surprise—are total lies. There can be no doubt about this.

If the leaders of America are proven to be liars, why are they allowed to continue in authority? Because the entire government is collaborating on a gargantuan lie that it is operating in the best interests of the America, when it is crystal clear it is not.

And that is precisely what leads us to this "Dead Zone" scenario. We know, from the perspective of history, what results Hitler was allowed to perpetrate because no one had the foresight or courage to stop this demented dictator before he pillaged most of Europe. If no one does anything now about Bush and his designs on world conquest, will we reap the same harvest? Will the entire world be consumed in torrents of depleted uranium flames? It seems very likely that it will.

What will we do when we finally realize we have the reincarnation of Hitler on our hands? Bush even venerates Hitler memorabilia that is kept by his college fraternity. Will we stop the madman in Washington, or will we let him have his way?

I myself do not believe in the death penalty for any reason, not even for a proven lover of capital punishment and mass murder such as George W. Bush. I guess that's how I'm different from virtually all the leaders of the so-called free world, who now generally approve of killing thousands of innocent Iraqi children in order to divvy up that beleaguered nation's oil reserves among themselves.

Despite their superficial protestations of "let the inspections work before we bomb them," none of them really measures the situation in terms of babies with birth defects or mothers who have to watch their children die of easily curable diseases because U.S. sanctions prevent doctors in Iraq from obtaining even the most basic kinds of medicine. None of them assesses the current crisis in terms of lives to be lost. In their crass calculations of budgets and political influence, human life is valueless to them. All that seems to matter to them is control of commodities, and kowtowing to the wishes of Israel, which manipulates the U.S. like a puppet to achieve its own aspirations to empire.

I wouldn't want to be like them. I pity them. If this is our future—if this is the way humans are supposed to behave—well, I guess this is not my kind of planet. As my old friend Guido, just past 90 and still messing with the authorities, says: "Once a person is dead, there's nothing you can do. All those possibilities of a long life lived, those connections, those achievements, those relatives, those inventions, they're gone, and the world is a lesser place."

This all seems so obvious to most thinking, feeling people. So obvious it's not even necessary to state it. Yet it's a thought that apparently escapes the thinking of our erstwhile leaders. So who are they, and who are we to let them ignore it?

And all this talk about "beginning" a war against Iraq is equally repellent to me. Sometimes, when I'm walking down the street, I want to run up to some businessman, grab him by the shirt, and scream: "Do you realize we've killed a million Iraqi children?!"

Do YOU realize the United States has killed a million Iraqi children in the last decade?

So, that's why I don't take kindly to talk about STARTING another war against Iraq, because the first war has never really stopped.

But conceding how many Iraqis America has already killed is not something the froth-mouthed George W. Bush would readily admit to. He's just not that kind of person.

All he's interested in doing is creating a "Dead Zone" of his own, a whole series of them actually. Of course, recruiting a Johnny Smith to cut short his career wouldn't solve the problem, because there are plenty of pathetic political poltergeists willing to walk in Bush's shoes and pursue his identical objectives, in which ordinary humans just don't count for much. Just look at who's next in line: our own Dr. Strangelove, Dick Cheney, the one person in the world who can make George W. Bush look like a humanitarian.

For that matter, just look at the situation now unfolding in Iowa caucuses, look at the so-called opposition party. More Bush clones, all willing to push that button and bomb Baghdad on the bogus basis of the lies that have been in place for a decade now. Gephardt, Kerry—all those pseudo-Democrats except Kucinich—would all eagerly step into Bush's shoes and continue this assault on humanity and common sense, ordering the needless deaths of thousands more brown-skinned innocents simply because the men who really push the buttons behind the scenes say this is the thing to do.

America is the new dead zone, morally and spiritually dead, where for some time now the price of gasoline has been a far more important topic than the lives of innocent people. That's what happened in the first Gulf War: America wholeheartedly endorsed the slaughter of 150,000 people in a few weeks just to keep the price of gasoline from rising too high.

Don't you realize the war in Iraq has never stopped? And don't you realize that if something seriously radical isn't done about the situation as it exists now, this new War on Terror is never going to stop? When Bush spoke at West Point two summers ago, he said there were 60 countries that harbored al-Qaeda terrorists.

If we don't stop him here and now, that's 60 wars we have to look forward to. Sixty new Dead Zones. The U.S. already has armed troops in 40 different countries. I guess that means we need a bigger defense budget, right?

I never thought I'd have to say this, but the "Dead Zone" scenario is real, not fiction. It's here and it's now. If the world ever regains any degree of real freedom and equanimity, I cringe at what the historians are going to say about us, and about how we let a man with the IQ of a pea roam around the world killing thousands for reasons that were so obviously lies.

Then the question remains: what do we do when confronted by the certainty of evil? Especially when the vast majority of the people in authority don't consider it to be evil, and have basically signed on to the evil course of action.

We need at least to remember that the people in power who endorse this plan of action, who endorse the cover-up of 9/11 and the abandonment of the anthrax investigation, who back the continuation of the attacks on hapless countries around the world, need to be separated from that authority as soon as possible. Immediately, if not sooner.

In our own distinctive ways, we all need to turn into Johnny Smiths, heed the unmistakable handwriting on the walls of our hearts, and take our own kind of action—humane and compassionate but effective action—to stop this menace that threatens to destroy the world as we know it.

To motivate yourself, simply consider the alternative if no action is taken. It's right there in the history books.

25

Heads they win, tails we lose

Lately I have involved myself in topics about which I seem to offend partisans on both sides of the same question.

As a journalist, this gives me great satisfaction, because true objectivity demands constructive criticism of both sides of any given issue, and in this I often succeed. But as a human being, it frustrates me that everybody from all points of the political spectrum can be so blindly biased; so unwilling to admit their own faults; so profoundly dense not to see that other people's arguments are often the same as their own though couched in different terms; so lacking in understanding, empathy, and fairness; so selfishly parochial as a new unprecedented worldwide disaster closes in on us.

Like, why should the United States have the right to declare other nations not suited to possess weapons of mass destruction? Or, why should one country have them (Israel) and another country not (Iraq)?

Does it all hinge on Condoleezza Rice's statement that we are a nation of truth and goodness and can determine what is right for everyone? And what of those who disagree? Are they wrong? Are they evil? Isn't the United States the country most likely to use weapons of mass destruction?

No wonder there are so many wars. Everybody says they're listening, but nobody's hearing anything, because everyone's consciousness is set up in such a way that they believe they are right, and anybody who says anything else is automatically an evil enemy. Objectivity seems to be an impossibility, determined entirely by those who control the methods of communication.

This process of getting caught in the middle of these kinds of arguments and being blasted from both sides regularly happens to me because I consort with people from all sections of the political spectrum, from pistol packing Patriots to grandmoms eager to lay in the street in front of tanks. Both groups, the nobility of whose motives are not really to be questioned, routinely fall into the careless use of stereotypes to characterize the nefarious forces they believe oppress them.

The Patriots call the Clintons Communists when they are actually cynical stooges for corporate totalitarians, and the lefties tag those on the way-right as selfish gun-toting racists when they are actually arguing for principles that would enrich all our lives.

But seen from a slightly different angle, those same Patriots (and libertarians, too) become shills for those very processes that now threaten to plunge the world into the darkness of war, and liberal lefties—who preach that if we all don't make it to freedom and security, none of us are going to make it—are all too often oblivious to the destruction of individual rights that they themselves espouse in their political campaigns. Never the twain seems to meet.

Anyway, the latest tar baby that has attached itself to my butt involves really kind of a toss-off line I used in my last essay about "The Dead Zone," when I waxed poetic that I was sitting on the shore of Vichy France waiting for the American bombers to arrive and change the nature of the world. To those certain few of my e-penpals who have identified with my previous critiques of Israel's fascist behavior throughout recent decades, it was as if I'd blasphemed the messiah.

How could I denigrate Hitler, when he was clearly a victim of the Western chapter of the worldwide Jewish conspiracy which set him up to take the big fall?

Whoa, Nellie! Just because I happen to believe in that worldwide Jewish conspiracy doesn't mean I have to believe that the little feller with the funny mustache and rigid arm was a good guy. I mean, nobody made him invade France, Poland, Czechoslovakia and all those other countries. Nobody made him preach a gospel of racial superiority (that now, very oddly, seems to have been adopted by the Jews) and herd his little coterie of black-uniformed twits into venom-spewing, hate-mongering robots out to obliterate the rest of the world.

No conspiracy made him do that. He took the ball and ran with it.

Just because I believe that Western business interests have manipulated worldwide markets and armies into numerous wars doesn't make me a fan of someone who wanted to take over the world.

But the real reason I can't identify with Hitler is that I can see from his philosophical descendants that he was pure, insane evil. And who are those philosophical descendants? Well, they are the Bush family, tied into the Hitler legacy through the second Bush president's forebears, Herbert Walker and Prescott Bush, who both made millions off their backing of German businesses during World War II. This is no fiction. Do a Google search. It's easy to find. These are Hitler's real philosophical descendants: the pro-war, Zionist Christian Republican establishment.

The Nazi legacy was passed to the conquering Americans through the CIA and the Dulles brothers, and the American space program, which wouldn't have succeeded without the help of German scientists. Nazi principles live on in the American corporate establishment, which condones absolutely anything in the name of profit and now has been given its favorite Nazi gift: the indefinite imprisonment (or even murder) of mere suspects without trial or appeal.

Yes, I can believe there was funny stuff going on prior to World War II involving Jewish control of the media and the financial markets that uncannily reflects what is going on now. I know about the implications of the Balfour Declaration: Germany would have won World War I, except that Jewish interests got the U.S. to enter the war after Britain made a secret promise to Zionists that they could have Palestine. But no, despite what was major provocative Jewish propaganda against him, I still believe Hitler was a white racist bent on destroying anybody who didn't have the kind of genetic heritage he preferred (and didn't even possess himself).

But just because I revile Hitler doesn't mean I believe the grandiose fictions the Jewish dominated media have spun about the Holocaust. I have been driven irrevocably into the category of Holocaust denier (a 1947 AP story said 875,000 Jews were killed in Germany during WW II) simply because of the way the Jewish community has trumpeted its martyrdom for financial gain, how the Jewish community has destroyed freedom of speech in a dozen European countries by making it a crime to talk about the events that led up to World War II.

I mean, if what the Jews were saying were actually true, they wouldn't need to pass laws to prevent their opponents from talking about it. They'd simply defeat them in an empirical argument, or in a court of law.

But to pass laws about talking about the events of World War II . . . I mean, that's almost as bad as George W. Bush preventing a thorough investigation into the events of 9/11/2001. It's a certain admission of guilt, an undeniable indication of a falsehood being perpetrated.

I submit the degree to which a reader of this may be horrified by this pronouncement is exactly the degree to which this same reader has been indoctrinated by media myths that severely alter the truth.

And when you realize that the Jewish community has stamped out freedom of speech throughout much of Europe, you naturally have to ask what that same group has done to legitimate political debate in the United States of America.

Back in World War II, there never was much coverage about how Eisenhower treated two million Germans in French prison camps that didn't even have buildings or latrines, an event surely as shameful as German concentration camps. Much has been said by partisans on both sides of this sorry episode, but Germans believe many of their innocents were unnecessarily killed in an act as vicious as anything else that happened in the war.

It's more of the same today. Nothing on TV or the big newspapers about the investigations into 9/11 or the anthrax murders, no coverage of the Palestinians being caged up in prison camps and murdered indiscriminately by bulldozers and helicopters on a daily basis, and not an audible peep about how it is Israel that has violated U.N. mandates about weapons of mass destruction and inhuman treatment of political prisoners.

Yet the U.S. gives Israel so much money ($14 billion per year) that it has begun to tip over the entire American economy, and still not a peep in the American mass media . . . because it is totally controlled by Jewish interests. This is not an exaggeration, no matter what trendy, left-leaning mass media observers like FAIR have to say about it.

But that still doesn't mean I have to like Hitler, or think he was right about anything, least of all Aryan superiority.

Same deal with Saddam. I can rail against how unjust and immoral the continuing target practice against Iraq is without saying anything nice about the Iraqi leader. Hell, the worst thing I can say about him was that he was a partner of the Bush family in acquiring weapons of mass destruction for his war against the truly legitimate democracy of Iran.

So, the Nazis say I'm soft on Israel because I don't like Hitler, and Jews call me an anti-Semite because I don't like Israeli soldiers putting bullets through the heads of old ladies and little babies. Everywhere I look I'm busted.

Anti-Semite. Hah. That's a laugh.

As many observers have written recently, an anti-Semite used to mean someone who hated Jews because they were Jews. Now, the term anti-Semite is used by Jews to tar and feather anyone who disagrees with Jewish policies, influences, and effects.

Complain about Israelis burying alive Palestinian residents of Jenin and Jews say you're an anti-Semite. Wonder about the preponderance of Jewish influence on the American government and you're an anti-Semite.

Worst of all were the recent remarks by Harvard president Lawrence Summers and his henchman Alan Dershowitz, who decried the recent rise of anti-Semitism. All this means to me is that Harvard is no longer a great university, but just another influential vehicle for Jewish propaganda. Check out the school's Enron investments sometime.

It's not a rise of anti-Semitism; it's a rise of disgust by thoughtful people who are appalled by the Jewish failure to admit the appalling crimes against humanity their Israeli cousins are perpetrating against the dark-skinned peoples of the region, and their political double agents are doing to the integrity of the American government.

This is a smokescreen kind of lie in which Jews exploited the so-called Holocaust for a kind of political immunity. Let's be nice to them because they've had a hard time, everyone was encouraged to think. And now we have more of the same: claims of a worldwide wave of anti-Semitism used to camouflage obvious genocide in the Middle East.

I'm not an anti-Semite. I'm anti-Israel, an illegal nation which has inherited all the worst traits of Hitler's regime and passed them onto the United States. And I'm anti-Jew because there are so few Jews with the honesty to admit their beloved sanctuary of Israel is a lethal menace to every decent nation and ethnic group on earth, including itself. This too is a Jewish legacy that has been successfully passed to the United States.

Anti-Semite. That's a good one.

Jews aren't Semites at all; they're Turkic Mongols, who stormed their way across Asia with Genghis Khan 1500 years ago, became Khazars in the Ukraine a thousand years ago, adopted Judaism as a political strategy, then infiltrated eastern Europe, always ashamed of their Oriental lineage, which they have done their best to conceal.

But it's no secret; they're still behaving like Genghis Khan, taking what they want and lying about it. They picked up a lot of good pointers from Hitler, that's all. They have become like Hitler, but they always were like Hitler, because they're a lot like Genghis Khan, the greatest butcher of all time (although the Bushes are in the running), because they're descended from him.

It's a terrible hoax, just like the Holocaust. Zionists had an office at Hitler's headquarters to funnel a "chosen" few to Palestine. And because Zionists controlled the American media, we fell for the myth of the Holocaust, although it wasn't really introduced into the public until 20 years after the war ended. Just like we're falling for it now—Israel freedom fighters against Palestinian terrorists. Hah. Israelis are stealing Palestinian land. They, and we, are the real terrorists.

America, controlled by Israel, is the genuine terrorist threat, just like the Christian crusaders of long ago were the real terrorists butchering the indigenous inhabitants of Arabia and India. Just look at any of the current polls. The whole world knows the real axis of evil: America, Britain and Israel, trying to bribe the whole world into seeing things in their ugly way. Everybody knows this except the American people, who are kept in the dark by Jewish media.

We are the real terrorists, people. Time to wake up.

Having said all this, I can't fault the Jews for being to any great degree worse than anyone else. Consider the Europeans, from whom most of you reading this are descended. Consider the European heritage from an American Indian perspective.

Who are the real killers now? Who are the true manipulators now? Pass out the smallpox blankets, people. Just plead guilty and take the deal. It's too late to argue. The verdict has been in for more than a century. It's just that you don't hear it because the media are all controlled by Europeans and Jews, trying hard to tell us what great folks we are, and how we have the right to destroy the world in order to rule. Just like Genghis Khan. We are all descended from Genghis Khan. Or Charlemagne. Same difference.

I don't have to prove any of this to anyone, because I don't want to kill anyone to defend a deep dark secret, and they do. They want to kill to take what they want so they can keep their deep dark secret.

The deep dark secret is that Israelis have no business whatsoever being in the Middle East at all.

Nothing gets fixed until the secret gets exposed. The secret is this: there are no colors and no nationalities. We are all members of the same tribe. Those who establish differences are just trying to make money off conflict. It's no more complex than that.

But in this game of political roulette happening right now on the eve of World War III, it's just a case of heads they win, tails we lose. It's a coin flip we can't win. The minute you turn on the TV or open a well-known newspaper, the game is fixed. Reasons to kill are plentiful and continually repeated: "They hate our freedom."

I'm going to lose the argument no matter what I say, because everyone has been conditioned to believe there has to be good and there has to be evil. No one—or damn few, anyway—have even considered the possibility that the striving for this "good" is the very thing that creates the "evil."

Consider this conversation I had with two schoolteachers the other night. Of course, I managed to offend both of them. One asked me what to do about children he could not reach, because they were only interested in computer-game retribution and seeing things in black and white.

I told him he wouldn't gain their confidence until he convinced them he believed there was a conspiracy against them. Silence followed. All teenagers know there's a conspiracy against them. They feel like adults but they're treated like kids. It's only the adults who pretend there isn't a conspiracy. And there is a conspiracy: kids are honest, adults are not. These same adults are the ones who wave the flag and support war.

Get this straight. The kids are right. There is a conspiracy against them.

And against us, too.

I can argue till I'm blue in the face that the human race has been conditioned to look to war and conflict as a way to solve its problems, but until each one of us in an actualized way realizes that we die and are not going to some holy place in the sky because we've exterminated those we've decided are infidels or enemies, nothing is going to get fixed, no message of peace—no matter how articulate and compassionate—is ever going to get through to us, because we're always going to have that enemy to be vanquished—even though the true enemy is always ourselves.

My response was greeted with uncomfortable silence. I had given them the right answer, but they couldn't even hear it. It made me wonder what myths they would actually teach.

So this is how I manage to offend people on both sides of the same issue. I like to think it's good journalism, which is more important to me than whether you like me, or agree with me.

And damn! I think I've just done it again.

26

Thomas Jefferson calling

The time for revolution is now

"*Prudence, indeed, will dictate that governments long established, should not be changed for light and transient causes; and, accordingly, all experience [has] shown that mankind are more disposed to suffer while evils are sufferable than to right themselves by abolishing the forms to which they are accustomed. But, when a long train of abuses and usurpations, pursuing invariably the same object, evinces a design to reduce [the people] under absolute despotism, it is their right, it is their duty, to throw off such government, and to provide new guards for their future security.*"

"*Rebellion to tyrants is obedience to God.*"

—Two quotes from Thomas Jefferson

Have you noticed? America is on the wrong side of every conflict in the world.

America encourages slavery and economic exploitation, and opposes individual rights and people's self determination—everywhere in the world. And now, with its new hardcore police-state laws, even in America itself.

No more the land of the free and home of the brave. That's long gone. Now it's the land of the financially pulverized and the home of grotesquely overpaid executroids who will say anything for the right price. Lie to anyone, friend or foe. Betray anyone for those thirty pieces of silver. Bribe other countries in order to get them to do things that everybody realizes are wrong. Poison its own soldiers because somebody makes billions getting rid of nuclear waste. Even kill a lot of its own citizens with medicines that are never tested, and protect the vicious felons who distribute these poisons from shattered parents mourning their dead children. Judasland, that's the America we have now.

Americans don't tell the truth to anyone, least of all themselves. And I direct this at not just the government, but also at the American people.

Y'know, it's easy to say we've been victimized by bad schools and coma-inducing TV, disgustingly manipulative movies, and a climate of elitist intolerance reflected in one-sided media versions of history.

It's one thing to be deceived, but it's quite another not to have seen all these crimes that have happened right in front our eyes since the Kennedy assassination. I mean: How stupid are we?

How stupid are we to believe that on one day in 2001, we had no air defenses for the entire Northeast region of the country? And that just happened to be the day when "terrorists" decided to fly four big jetliners into national landmarks. As Gerard Holmgren so eloquently said recently, how stupid are we to believe a conspiracy theory as far-fetched as that, one that was engineered by disaffected Arabs in a cave? See http://www.911-strike.com/debunking.htm

So, yes, we can keep blaming our bad luck and lack of attention to political reality, but let's not forget to blame ourselves in all this. And blame ourselves right now for not already having stopped an entire Congress intent on covering up the most important event of our lives, and then timidly approving the wars of our new dictator who seeks to keep the population deceived with one murderous escapade after another.

How stupid are we to believe all of it? Or any of it?

How stupid are we not to know the stock market crashed months ago and is being propped up by the Plunge Protection Team?

How stupid are we not to know that nothing the Bush Administration says remotely resembles an honest assessment of conditions in the world. All those satanic shills say is designed to ease their task of stealing money from people everywhere.

Recently many high profile Americans have been caught in embarrassing lies. Although the media tries to cover them as best they can, more and more people are noticing that everything the Bush administration says is a spin, and none of it is an honest recounting of actual events.

If Powell and Bush are telling lies now about reasons to invade Iraq—and getting caught at those lies regularly—how are we to know that they weren't telling lies about the demolition of the World Trade Center, when it was considered unpatriotic to question the official version of events?

If they're lying now, what kind of stupid do you have to be to believe they were telling the truth then? Pretty stupid, is what I'd say.

I bet it's just hysterical when Poppy Bush, Cheney and Rumsfeld get together and laugh about how efficiently they've ripped off the American people. Cheney can brag that Halliburton, through its Brown & Root subsidiary, had made trillions off all these frequent U.S. military deployments in which his company provides the crappy chow and the tossed-up buildings. With plenty more of those lucrative military support contracts to follow in quick succession. North Korea.

Philippines. Colombia. You pick the target.

And Bush 41 can laugh right back by bragging about how many anthrax tablets and smallpox doses his new company Bioport has foisted off on the government. It's doesn't matter that they'll never be used by anyone with a scintilla of common sense. The deal is done and the money has been paid. If anyone actually gets the shot, well, that's their tough luck.

For at least a century, the whole world has emulated America, presidents instead of dictators, legislatures instead of secret police. Now America has reverted to the secret police method. Woe to everyone if the world continues to follow America's lead. With its cooked-book capitalism, where nothing is the truth and all but richest suffer, America is leading the world over a cliff, and pushing the world toward that precipice too with weapons that couldn't be surpassed by the devil himself in their high-tech evil.

America stands for total corporate control with no discussion and no dissension, and against meaningful self-expression and common sense ways to ease the burdens of the less fortunate. Virtually no members of Congress oppose open U.S. aggression in dozens of foreign countries. And neither, for that matter, do many foreign leaders, our erstwhile allies, most of whom are on the U.S. bribery payroll.

And America is raising its children in this manner, too, which is why you see so few kids at peace demonstrations compared to the number of people with white hair. Something to look forward to—a totally robotized next generation. But this is far from the most disturbing trend in America today.

More importantly, America is against saving the environment, preferring instead to just trash it and then try to make even more money off the cleanup. Focused totally on the bottom line, America practices poisoning the oceans and the jungles of the world on the theory that these places are far away and don't pertain directly to immediate profits.

But almost all of these so-called leaders and a disturbing percentage of the general population applaud these empty lies America uses to ravage the planet. They listen to the TV fascists and believe what they hear. They see themselves getting richer from these selfish, shortsighted policies, without realizing they are becoming immensely poorer.

Most of the rest of the world is beginning to realize that America is against what is morally right and sociologically sound, and in favor of what benefits the rich controllers at the expense of the poor, no matter how many people these policies kill. In fact, since it happens in so many countries, America seems to prefer policies that kill a lot of people.

Roll that over in your mind. America prefers killing large numbers of people, the more different ways the better.

Afghanistan: 10,000 dead and more dying every day from incredibly high levels of radioactivity that almost certainly came from the U.S. use of nuclear weapons, which of course nobody will admit using. All of those people were, of course, innocent of anything except trying to eke out a hardscrabble living in a spot where a bunkerbuster bomb happened to be dropped.

Iraq: 1.5 million dead in 10 years from illegal bombing by the U.S. and Britain, but the truly heartrending part is all the children that have needlessly died because sadistic sanctions kept basic medicines from doctors treating kids with very ordinary illnesses. It is for this most Americans deserve to go straight to hell.

Colombia: Now they drop the poison rain to get the peasants to move off land that American corporations want to develop, a fine climax to 30 years of war America has waged through its proxy goons while nobody in the U.S. noticed.

Remember: America has armed troops in 40 different countries, and all this horrific stuff is going on there, too. How many Guatemalan peasants are buried in the mud of unmarked graves because American corporations wanted to prevent a "Communist" threat?

Remember: Bush set up a secret government and didn't even bother to tell the Democrats. And now he laughs at millions of people opposing his policies in the streets, and calls them "a focus group" not to be trusted.

America insists upon one set of permissive rules for itself, and another set of restrictive rules for everybody else, which is why it refuses to allow itself to be ruled by the auspices of any world court. This is clearly a racist elitism, a plantation mentality, a neverending extension of the continuing colonialist rape of the world.

America looks down its nose at the rest of the world. Any legitimately unbiased world court would find America guilty of innumerable counts of tyranny in a heartbeat. In fact, the list of indictable offenses, acts of aggression, extortion, espionage, violations of the Geneva Accords and crimes against humanity would probably occupy such a world court indefinitely into the foreseeable future.

That day will come. When the playing field of the world gets leveled, as it inevitably will, America faces an endless succession of war crimes charges in just about every country on earth, from rapes in Okinawa to mass murder by smallpox injection in the Congo.

Which is just what Malaysian Prime Minister Mahathir Mohamed was saying the other day at the summit of Non-Aligned Nations in Kuala Lumpur. The "uncertainties of today's world are due not to 'a clash of civilizations' between the West and Islam, but to a revival of the old European trait of wanting to dominate the world. The expression of this trait invariably involves injustices and oppression of people of other ethnic origins and colours. It is no longer just a war against terrorism. It is, in fact, a war to dominate the world."

How many Americans have asked: What right does America have to say other countries may not have weapons to defend themselves equal to what America has? Did some God appoint America to rule the world? Are we to believe the black quisling Condoleezza Rice when she says America has the best interests of the world at heart?

Many Asians, wrote journalist Andre Vltchek, feel that it is not just the UN that Bush threatens to make irrelevant. It is the entire world that is not white, the entire world that strives to remain culturally different and opposes the world order and one-way globalisation.

How could it be that a country that made its reputation on democracy and individual liberties is now an inflexible totalitarian system bent on bringing every person on earth under its oppressive fist, either through irresistible bribes to corrupt leaders, outright invasions, or the imposition of devastating financial shackles through that economic shell game known as the International Monetary Fund?

It's a simple answer, really.

America has never been a legitimate democracy and is not one now. From many of the founding fathers who argued against unbridled democracy during a time where less than a quarter of its citizens were authorized to cast a vote, through two centuries of continuing consolidation of power by corporate interests, the legends that anyone can rise to be president or the U.S. is a real system of one person/one vote have been exposed as populist myths, imbedded in an entire curriculum of myths that have led the populace to believe that America is an honest and just nation.

For many years, to those in other countries under the yoke of barbaric dictators, the U.S. seemed—from far away—to LOOK like a democratic system, with all its ceremonial rituals of supposedly representative government, with its Constitution and Bill of Rights. But a closer look—for most, limited to the writings of many poorly publicized and little known social critics—has always revealed a superficial democratic sideshow masking the same inhumane system of bribery and extortion that rules all nations.

Now, once again, the world is being shown the real deal.

Once known as the world's greatest democracy, America still pretends to preach a gospel of freedom, but look at its allies: blatant tyrannies which survive on American payoffs and rob and kill their own people. These police state allies are always headed by puppet dictators who are approved and appointed by American business interests. Just look at proposed U.S. plans for a future Iraqi "democracy," to be temporarily headed by a former American general. Most Americans can't even recall the number of times the U.S. has tinkered with Iraqi "democracy" in the past.

It's easy to see all this if you just look, but the vast majority of Americans choose not to.

You simply have to observe how America must bribe its so-called allies to get them to go along with repressive policies. America thinks it can buy its friends. What a horrible price we shall all pay for this in the future. Imagine the resentment building in every corner of the globe as people realize they are not allowed to think for themselves in order to continue receiving pathetic pittances of America's trickle down largesse. Ask the once-middle-class families now living in the streets of Argentina about this.

America attempted to solve the crisis in the Middle East by giving billions of dollars to Egypt in exchange for a promise not to invade Israel. The majority of Egyptians disagree with this policy, but Egypt's leaders have instituted a police state that prevents people from expressing their own beliefs. America funnels trillions to Saudi Arabia while a majority of that country's citizens chafe under an inflexible, capricious dictatorship that spends a lot of money in Monte Carlo.

This is the kind of "democracy" the U.S. now wishes to inflict on Iraq. America wants to create another flunkie regime to do its bidding, another fake democracy to advance the anti-democratic cause of American banks and oil companies. Just like the fake democracy in America.

America has bombed Iraq for 13 years and claimed it is not at war. Now, it prepares to obliterate the entire population of that country simply to steal oil fields and provide a better supply of water for Israel. And to gain a staging area for invasions of other countries.

America enthusiastically endorses the genocide of the Palestinian people knowing full well Israel is an illegal entity forced on the indigenous inhabitants against their will, just like many other Mideast nation-states.

America is now ready to invade Colombia after supporting the destruction of the people for three decades so it can better control the importation of oil and cocaine. This aggression will likely explode over the borders into neighboring countries.

America uses business executives to bribe the people of Venezuela to overthrow their own democratically elected government, and claims it is advocating democracy.

America continues to support corporate-connected dictators in most Central American countries, and resorts to mass murder when popular movements agitate for justice for poor people. America is so proud of this longstanding colonialist policy that it promoted one of the chief executors of this strategy, John Negroponte, to U.S. ambassador to the United Nations, sending a message to the whole world that it intends to treat all other countries just like Guatemala, Nicaragua, and El Salvador: either accept corporate control over your slavery or you'll wind up face down in the mud.

America is sending troops to the Philippines to suppress a popular uprising that seeks democratic control over a corrupt government that is totally subservient to U.S. business interests. No wonder Muslim idealists want to get rid of it.

America even manages to make the Taliban look good. The fundamentalist Muslim fanatics had all but wiped out poppy production, but now, thanks to the new American-backed government, under the tutelage of new Republican DEA chief Asa Hutchinson, it's thriving and Afghanistan is now the world's No. 1 producer of heroin that finds its way to the streets of Europe.

You can't argue that these international intrigues are necessary for America's economic survival when $4.5 TRILLION has gone missing from the federal coffers in Washington in just the last two years with no explanation. The basic situation in Washington is that a cabal of petronazis has managed to change all the laws in order to facilitate the greatest robbery in human history, which is now underway.

I could go on, of course, but the questions I get most are: What to do? Unfortunately, I keep coming with what not to do.

- Don't send petitions to your elected representatives. Most of them are involved in the robbery, and have no interest in liberating American citizens from corporate totalitarianism because they making too much money taking bribes. Even many of the ones who say they do really don't; they're just placating voters. Ask the people who write letters to phony shills like John Kerry and Diane Feinstein; they never get an answer that isn't some kind of vacuous form letter.
- Impeachment attempts? Give me a break. Same deal. Virtually the entire Congress is on the take. Were any congressperson to back an impeachment, he or she would be jeopardizing their own criminal income from the corporate conspiracy. When the day of retribution comes, all elected representatives and senators who either voted for the Patriot Act or took contributions from Enron should automatically be thrown in jail, and held indefinitely under terms of the Patriot Act for consorting with known terrorists (in this case, George W. Bush and Kenneth Lay).

Still, in thousands of e-mails, that big question keeps coming: What will we do to keep from becoming residents of Camp Ashcroft?

Well, here's your answer.

Overthrow the government — NOW

We must overthrow the government. There is no other choice. Nothing else will work. Could it be more obvious?

We can't use violence, because real humans would be crushed by all the hellish weapons arrayed against the entire world by the military industrial complex that has stolen all our money and erased all our rights under the Constitution.

Besides, it is illegal under what's left of the Constitution to advocate the VIOLENT overthrow of the government. And I would never dream of advocating any such thing.

It is, however, patently legal and indeed our patriotic duty to advocate the peaceful overthrow of the government.

We have to overthrow the government, just like Jefferson said, in a fit of moral outrage, using every bit of our wits and our influence to put these people who are in the process of destroying everything we hold dear in jail. For a long time, if not forever.

We must demand the president and his evil entourage resign and present themselves for criminal indictments before a newly constituted citizens court that is not influenced by the big bucks of big business.

We need to restore America to the republic it was designed to be and the democracy it claims to be.

What?! Are you going to wait for the next election? The elections are all fixed by electronic voting machines and corporate media that actually change the way people think.

The Congress must resign as well, and most of them are eligible for indictment, too. Anyone who voted for the first Patriot Act without reading must be charged with treason, for destroying our rights without cause, and anyone who has ever taken a campaign contribution from Enron (or any of a host of other criminal corporations) must be charged with corruption and receiving stolen property, namely, the people's money.

And of course the entire judiciary must resign, and a new judiciary reappointed by the new government.

All this doesn't have to happen all at once. That would probably be unworkable.

Somebody else can figure out how to conduct new elections—without the electoral college—later. The first thing to be done is to remove the cancer immediately, before it's too late. There are enough responsible people in America to decide democratically what kind of interim administration should coordinate a transitional government until new elections can be called.

There are also a very few responsible existing legislators like Ron Paul and Dennis Kucinich who can help facilitate the transition.

There are those who would protest that this is too radical an idea, too big to be considered, too shocking to ever gain a hold in the popular imagination. But I submit there is nothing else to be done. We must demand they resign and make it stick. Otherwise, we are lost. Because there is no fixing this corrupt system. And to not fix it is to throw away the future of the human species.

This is a preposterous idea, you undoubtedly sputter and fume. How could it possibly work, you inquire incredulously?

Here's how.

Twenty million people converge on Washington and demand the resignation of the entire government, that's how. I'd like it to be on July 4, 2003, but it can't be, because all those phony politicos are out of town fishing or in Vegas gambling our money away, or wherever.

We have to catch them actually in Washington, Congress in session, President in the White House, Cheney in his bunker or wherever he actually hangs out. Responsible representatives must serve them with subpoenas and arrest warrants.

We have to mob our nation's capital with so many people that they will have no alternative but to step down.

And there has to be so many people that they can't even contemplate arresting anyone. I mean, where are you going to detain 20 million people?

Why 20 million? I don't know the right number, but I know one million isn't enough, because there have been several million-person gatherings—Farrakhan's, the Moms, the Christian guys—and they barely elicited a ripple from the establishment.

So it has to be a number that will be absolutely impossible to ignore. Twenty million, I figure, should do it.

Where would everyone stay? And what would they eat? I submit the African-American community will take us in, assist us, lead us in strategically positioning ourselves all over Washington so that the disgusting perps can't get away. Plus, with such an outpouring of people from all over America, I believe the cops would come over to our side, the side of the people, against the side of the tyrants. After all, cops really aren't tyrants; they're people too.

It's not impossible. Hell, there are 20 million people in metropolitan New York; there have to be 50 million in the greater Northeast alone. But if this thing were really to come down, people would come from everywhere. The U.S. population is 290 million. Hell, 20 million is less than 10 percent, but I think it would be enough to get their attention, shut down the entire Northeast Corridor and force the corrupt sociopaths to call it quits.

The reason I think this will actually work is the makeup of people I've seen at protests all across the land. The protests have not consisted of a single age, ethnic or religious group; not a single race or political splinter group. There has been a tremendous cross-section of the American population, and I think this augurs positively for 20 million to come to Washington and simply demand that the criminals step down and submit to the charges of people's warrants for treason and obstruction of justice, among many others.

Can we get 20 million? Maybe not. However, as conditions continue to deteriorate in this country and more people find themselves kicked to the curb after the stock market really crashes, I think it's realistic to expect this many people to want to participate.

If we can't get 20 million, maybe 10 million will do. And if we can't get enough to keep the cops from locking up all of us, well, then there was never any hope anyway. We might as well be arrested on the streets of Washington as wait in our homes for them to come and get us.

We use their own disgusting labels against them, categorizing politicians like they're now segregating airline passengers into red, yellow, and green classes. The green ones get to help us, the yellow ones get subpoenas and the red ones go right to jail. We should let that fabulous class of black rappers, who have been righteously commenting for so long on the infernos that are our cities, do the categorizing.

Among the provisions in this operation to be designed would be a one-step lockup process, much like they use for illegal immigrant roundups, that would funnel the most egregious governmental criminals right into a holding cell for a little diesel therapy. This group, of course, would include the president and his cabinet.

All of these people need to be held under the provisions of the Patriot Act, for which they themselves voted, which would deny them bond, access to counsel, or family visits, until an investigation into their crimes was completed. Yes, that could take a long time.

Think a revolution of unbridled moral outrage, really the only response that is called for by caring humans in our present situation.

So, people have asked me what to do. This is what we must do.

And we need to do it while we still can, because if they pass many laws like the two Patriot Acts, the opportunity to do it will be gone forever.

Let me ask you one question. Have you considered what will happen if we don't do this? As dangerous as this idea is, it's more dangerous not to do. They're already picking off people one at a time. A lawyer in New Mexico gets busted for saying in a chatroom that Bush is out of control.

A guy in a bar in South Dakota gets three years in jail for telling a joke about a burning Bush.

Those people languishing in Guantanamo for two years had nothing to do with the Taliban and were rounded up by Pakistani police on a bounty system so Rumsfeld could feel like a tough guy keeping innocent people in jail without having to bring them to trial.

The long ago words of Ben Franklin are appropriate here: "We either all hang together or we all hang separately." That's the way it is in a revolution.

As it stands now, America has no respect for anybody or anything, human or holy. America doesn't even respect itself, because it's too busy screwing people to steal their money and their resources.

The sad fact is—one which we will learn to our peril if not ultimate destruction—is that you can't respect yourself if you don't respect everybody else. So it's obvious America doesn't even respect itself anymore, because it sure doesn't respect anybody else in the world.

America is at war with the entire world. And most Americans choose not to believe it, even though it's happening right in front of their eyes. And as we speak, Americans are becoming the real victims of a tyranny they have permitted to grow to truly ominous proportions.

It's time to do something about it. Although massive logistical problems and ad hoc legal procedures need to be developed, this would work, I think. And Thomas Jefferson would like it a lot.

27

The dream in flames

Brave American pilots will show Iraqi children how it feels to be vaporized . . .

Dictator Bush and his wimpy quisling suckups at the *New York Times*, CNN, and Fox have proved that Adolf Hitler's strategy was right—if you tell a lie enough times it soon becomes the truth in the public mind.

And we see how this technique has now come full circle in this rerecorded non-debate about bombing Iraq into a deeper level of oblivion.

Remember late autumn 2002, when from seemingly out of nowhere Bush put the long-dormant Iraq issue back on the front burner? At the time the U.S. media were awash in stories about how many Americans would die from the president's ill-considered order to vaccinate the entire population for smallpox. That the president's father had just acquired a substantial interest in the company that was to make the vaccines never quite managed to make the front page.

The unsolved anthrax murders had already disappeared as a story from the mainstream media, once the trail of suspicion led straight to the U.S. government's door. A permanent *rigor mortis* had already set into the 9/11 probe and the unsolved sudden murders of more than 3,000 Americans. But Enron and Halliburton's troubles seemed to be percolating a bit, as many business executives who had stolen millions from innocent but greedy Americans seemed to be headed for embarrassing questions in various courts. It was not until later that a Bush-appointed appeals court judge's order would take the heat off Cheney for engineering that whole deal that stole billions in energy costs from the people of California. Cheney never liked California; he's a Wyoming boy.

What the criminal administration needed was a distraction from all this consternation, and Iraq has been that and more.

Now, not one of those overpaid media succubi who smirk on the TV screen every night and tell you America is going to win this war against Iraq has the gonads to tell their dictator that his planned invasion of that bomb-pocked nation breaks every law known to man and signed by the United States: the Geneva Accords, the Nuremburg agreements and every treaty civilized people have endorsed since the Romans bugged out of Britain—it is illegal to attack someone if they're not attacking you.

A pre-emptive war is not allowed by civilized people.

Hey, why would they ask such a question? It's only the reason why there's any peace in the world at all, that's why. You don't go around gunning down your neighbors because you think they're going to do something bad to you sometime in the future. Only a criminal psychopath would do something like that.

But the current president of the United States knows something more than all the diplomats in human history put together. After all, he says he's a religious man. And Jesus did say he brought not peace but a sword. That's George W. Bush's kind of religion. I'm sure you could convince him that somewhere in the Bible it says it's OK to obliterate anyone you suspect of having weapons of mass destruction even though you can't prove it. Wasn't that the rationale of the Biblical Israelites when they wiped out all those other tribes?

Or if it's not in the Bible, maybe those sophisticated designers of the Project for the New American Century, the ones who wrote America needed "a Pearl Harbor-type event" shortly before the World Trade Center came crashing down, can get it put in. Maybe in a new version of Deuteronomy 28:56–58, that part where God says mothers will have to eat their own children if they don't obey God's holy law, maybe Richard Perle and Paul Wolfowitz can change that to it's OK to nuke innocent families because their leader didn't obey orders from their masters to give them all the oil they wanted.

Probably most Christians wouldn't even notice the change. It's all about the collection plate, anyway.

Or I guess some religious people like the singing. Onward Christian Soldiers, marching off to war, with the cross of Jesus, going on before. Amen.

I heard the crosses they're taking to Iraq are made out of depleted uranium, too. A lot harder than gold. They can really smite the enemy with them, just like our drug czar, that Barry McCaffrey guy. You know he used to be a general and he was in charge of the operation that gunned down all those Iraqis trying to run away from Kuwait after the first Gulf War. They called it the "Highway of Death." A lot of American pilots thought it was just like a shooting gallery at an amusement park.

I don't know if they got points for it or not. McCaffrey became real famous for killing all those people who didn't have a chance, driving rusted-out trucks trying to escape American jets. He's a true American hero.

Yep, America's really going to put on a show. The American armed forces have the coolest high-tech weapons ever, and they've been saying—especially that Rumsfeld fellow—that they're going to use some new weapons nobody's ever seen before. I'll bet they'll be on TV, too. I wonder if CNN will make up a jingle like "Showdown with Iraq" to go along with Rumsfeld's plans to use "calmative agents" on the population of Baghdad, so as to reduce the resistance to American forces, y'know.

I can just imagine the new logo on Fox: "Gassing the masses." The ratings will probably be good.

Calmative agents. I like that term. Just like the Russians used on those Chechen terrorists who tried to hijack that Russian theater a while back. Just shot the gas in there and they all went to sleep. I think that's a big improvement in warfare, and Americans should be proud to use stuff like that. I mean, instead of dropping all these humongous bombs on people and blowing them to bits, just spread a little cloud of chemical smoke over them and put them all to sleep. That's a real improvement in warfare, and Americans should be real proud to use something like that. It makes war a lot more civilized. Just put 'em to sleep instead of blowing 'em to bits.

'Course the problem in Russia was that a lot of 'em didn't wake up.

But there'll still be bombs. Plenty of bombs that we'll watch on TV. Cameras right in the tips of the bombs. Ride 'em right down to the target. See all those buildings blow up. Cool. 'Course they don't show the people being blown up. They won't show the searing heat from those heralded U.S. laser-guided bombs incinerating the crinkled skin of already-sick Iraqi children. Try to imagine the sound that crackling would make and think of something appropriate for a U.S. military recruiting poster.

That wouldn't be right on TV. Hell, if you showed that, bodies flying apart and heads being blown off, the skin of little children crackling in flames, people wouldn't want to go to war at all, would they? Hell, we can't have that.

They also were going to use some kind of fancy bomb that knocked out everybody's electronics in the area it was used, but I think they ditched that idea when they figured it would also probably make all their own airplanes fall out of the sky.

But the best part, I think, the most effective form of warfare, is the depleted uranium ammunition, the gift that keeps on killing year after year after year.

Could anything be more illustrative of the top leadership in America being completely and certifiably insane than using ammunition that guarantees a bitter harvest of disease and death among its own troops for years to come? Consider the casualty factor from the first Gulf War.

Only 147 American personnel were killed during combat, a substantial number of those from accidental (we hope) friendly fire. But now, the Gulf War death toll 13 years later is around 10,000 Americans (if you check around on the Internet), with another 140,000 afflicted with really nasty diseases that are passed to those wives and children who manage to survive for any length of time.

Sure, you get the standard argument from the psycho U.S. government that these maladies are caused by other things, like the oil well fires (now alleged by some veterans to have been set by American personnel) and poison gas attacks. But the two main suspected carcinogenic culprits continue to be depleted uranium ammunition and strange vaccinations about which the U.S. government never would say and won't to this day what was actually in them. Go wave your damned American flag about that one, buddy.

America kills it own soldiers just by using DU ammunition. People get rich selling nuclear waste to ordnance manufacturers. And American soldiers die because of it. You can't deny it. There's too much evidence, everywhere.

Now we must return to the lead of our story: lies told often enough that they become the truth in the minds of an addled and distracted populace that wishes the whole story would just go away.

It is not Iraq that has weapons of mass destruction and uses them against its neighbors. It is the United States.

Compare the two nations. How many nations has Iraq invaded under its present leadership?

Answer: Two. First Iran, with the eager backing of the United States, which supplied it with chemical and biological weapons (and now proposes to use the same weapons to attack Iraq for using chemical and biological weapons of mass destruction). Second, Kuwait, which was stealing Iraqi oil, and anyway, the claim that it is a part of Iraq is legitimate; Kuwait, Iraq and Saudi Arabia were all created arbitrarily by the oil companies (as was Saudi Arabia).

Then, how many countries has America invaded and used weapons of mass destruction against during the same time period?

Answer: Try 14. Grenada 1983, Lebanon 1983, 1984 (both Lebanese and Syrian targets), Libya 1986, El Salvador 1980s, Nicaragua 1980s, Iran 1987, Panama 1989, Iraq 1991–2000, Somalia 1993, Bosnia 1994, 1995, Sudan 1998, Afghanistan 1998, Yugoslavia 1999. (Thanks to William Blum, *Rogue State: A Guide to the World's Only Superpower.*)

So when those mostly white men (they're all white at heart) gather around the table at the United Nations and make their judgment that Iraq needs to be invaded, they're just pulling out the same story that the Western powers have used ever since the Crusades were started to go and loot the dark-skinned natives. The lie is so colossal that it just makes me want to throw up.

When Americans—otherwise intelligent and kind—say Iraq should be invaded because they are connected with the 9/11 attacks—there is no recognized shred of evidence that this is so—it makes me want to throw up as well.

And when the world's media feign hysteria about Iraq being a menace to its neighbors—at the same time when not far away Israel is perpetrating one of the great genocides in human history, the erasing of the entire nation of Palestine, and because most newspapers are owned by Jews, no one is saying a word—it makes me want to . . . well, you know.

The world is, in fact, mad. Willfully and deliberately so.

People of principle need to assert themselves now. A poison has spread around the entire globe. Every echo of every thought emanating from virtually every radio station, television channel and major newspaper throughout the entire world (well, certainly the Western world, anyway) is a lie. And for this lie, thousands of people are being murdered every day.

The United Nations itself, consisting of representatives of all the countries on Earth, looks with favor on this newest lie, that Iraq is the threat to the world and needs to be divested of its leaders and its resources. So, the whole world agrees to participate in this lie, presumably in exchange for future political advantages from the aggressor government that seeks, as is its usual custom, to perpetrate this particular lie for its own geopolitical and financial gain, yet couches its motives in familiar phrases of perfunctory and insincere nobility.

The big news in this is that the whole world is agreeing to participate in the slaughter of innocents because the most powerful country wishes to perpetrate its continuing campaign of dishonest, imperialistic gambits in order to increase its wealth. There is no other reason.

The alpha dog wishes to destroy an entire nation, and the subservient pups that all other nations have become gather round, hoping to steal leftover scraps from the slaughter.

In all this, where are the principles of a free society of free people living in a free world? Where is the compassion that supposedly distinguishes humans from other animals? Where is the basic integrity of members of any society who agree to be civilized and not kill other people except in self-defense?

I'll tell you where they are. They're gone.

Of this event, our posterity will calculate the loss of our humanity and our honor, but in sociological terms, this complicity of the entire world to participate in this latest vigilante lynching of Iraq may well signal for us as a species the end of evolution and the beginning of entropy . . . and the long, slow slide toward an ignominious extinction.

The future of the whole world is mortgaged to the vicious caprice of the American police state. Honest men cower in their castles and calculate the cost of their betrayal of the human race. The dream is in flames.

Appendix

Best 9/11 Sites
4th Edition

If you were to read every story on every website mentioned in this post, we wouldn't hear from you for years.

However, if you were to scan all the sites mentioned here, and picked out stories that piqued your interest, something profound would happen. You would never trust what you read in your local newspaper or believe what you heard on TV ever again.

And that is exactly the point of this list.

The World Wide Web is where the genuine information is today. The mass media have deteriorated into a deceptive and delusional miasma of propaganda pitches designed not to tell the truth about current events, but to spin them in ways that will be profitable to the patricians who own the media outlets and pay for the deceptive advertising that ruin the health and fortunes of ordinary citizens who are just trying to live their lives in a peaceful and orderly manner.

Print and broadcast mass media are the agents of deception and delusion—no exceptions.

The corporate mainstream media are all colluding in a criminal obstruction-of-justice coverup with corrupt government officials who have morphed the United States of America from a relatively functioning democratic republic into a private plunder preserve for the rich where ordinary people are regularly robbed of their hard-earned money and the privileged yet uneducated elite are free to trash the resources of the world's most gifted nation and sell them to the highest bidder.

With the help of corrupt judges and conscienceless politicians, America has become the scourge of the world as it loots country after country at the same time it deprives its own citizens not only of their basic rights that were once protected by a functioning Constitution, but also of their security, their wealth, and their self-respect as scam after scam—drugs, wars, and products you don't need that don't work—are foisted on unsuspecting consumers.

The information contained on these websites will help you see things differently, and more accurately.

This is the fourth time I've compiled this list. Each time it has expanded and changed slightly. A few sites have dropped off. Many more have been added.

This list is only one person's opinion of what's out there on the web regarding information about the coverup of 9/11.

This list as meant as a recommendation of where to find valid information not curdled by corporate contempt.

It is not meant to be a complete list, and apologies to all those great sites out there I haven't found yet. I always like getting recommendations and I understand that what I like might not be what you like.

Nevertheless, after a year of surfing every day, these are the sites I've found to be most valuable. I would sincerely urge you to check all of them out at your leisure and support them financially if you are able.

Everything recommended on this list is free (although with some, you can get add-ons that do cost money). I have taken pains not to include any sites of an overtly religious or spiritual nature, being a believer in the following statement: Anytime an adherent of one religion says anything at all about another religion, it is not to be taken seriously because the speaker can't help but be completely biased, and is therefore unreliable.

I have also excluded the categories of economics and the law, because not being an economist or a lawyer, I'm not sure when I'm being bamboozled by fancy rhetoric and references to documents with which I am unfamiliar.

Best 9/11 Sites - 4th Edition*

Most important site:

http://www.copvcia.com/

Best news sources:

http://www.rense.com/
http://www.whatreallyhappened.com/
http://www.unansweredquestions.org
http://www.globalresearch.ca/
http://www.questionsquestions.net/ (See note at end.)
http://www.guerrillanews.com/
http://www.apfn.org/apfn/kenvardon.htm
http://www.communitycurrency.org/index.html
http://www.onlinejournal.com/
http://www.madcowprod.com/
http://www.tomflocco.com/

Best 9/11 timelines:

http://www.cooperativeresearch.org/home.htm
http://home.att.net/~Resurgence/CIAtimeline.html
http://www.911pi.com/

Best liberal leftie sites:

http://www.wsws.org/index.shtml
http://www.indymedia.org/(and many other indymedia affiliates)
http://www.legitgov.org/
http://www.iacenter.org/
http://www.freedomroad.org/home.html
http://www.yellowtimes.org/index.php
http://www.flybynews.com/
http://www.medialens.org/
http://www.zmag.org/
http://www.democracynow.org/

---

* www.GoOFF.com, the bookstore for Dandelion Books, publisher of this book (and the best spot for buying it) is not included in this rating. Launched less than a year ago, it has become one of the most popular and valuable websites for obtaining uncensored news and news digests.

Best Patriot right sites:

http://www.americanfreepress.net/
http://proliberty.com/observer/index.htm
http://www.public-action.com/
http://www.sierratimes.com/
http://www.savethemales.ca/index.html
http://www.thenewamerican.com/
http://www.globalist.org/

Best mainstream right sites:

http://www.lewrockwell.com/
http://www.antiwar.com/
http://www.senderberl.com/
http://www.etherzone.com/
http://www.larouchein2004.net/index.html
http://strike-the-root.com/

Best all-around analytical websites:

http://www.americanstateterrorism.com/AmericanStateTerrorism.html
http://www.hermes-press.com/index.html
http://www.ratical.org/ratville/JFK
http://www.sumeria.net/wnew.html
http://serendipity.magnet.ch/index.html
http://www.cooperativeresearch.org/index-old1.htm
http://www.assassinationscience.com/
http://www.911-strike.com/index.htm
http://davesweb.cnchost.com/
http://www.public-i.org/dtaweb/home.asp
http://www.thememoryhole.org/index.htm
http://www.thirdworldtraveler.com/Blum/US_Interventions_WBlumZ.html
http://www.lovearth.net/ (www.standdown.net)

Best site destroyed by the federales:

http://www.voxnyc.com/

Best site bought off by the Israelis:

http://www.emperors-clothes.com/

Best mind expanding websites:

http://www.conspiracyplanet.com/
http://www.davidicke.com/icke/index1a.html
http://www.skolnicksreport.com/
http://www.paranoiamagazine.com/
http://www.nexusmagazine.com/index.html
http://www.cloakanddagger.ca/home.asp
http://www.dcia.com/index.htm

Best elected official sites:

http://www.house.gov/lee/
http://www.house.gov/kucinich/
http://www.house.gov/paul/tst/welcome.htm

Best essays:

http://www.americanfreepress.net/09_03_02/NEW_SEISMIC_/new_seismic_.html
http://www.questionsquestions.net/kolskegg_911.html
http://www.narconews.com/goff1.html
http://www.sumeria.net/politics/bushknew/ghostriders.html
http://www.sumeria.net/politics/shadv3.html
http://www.afn.org/~vetpeace/madness.html
http://www.lannan.org/_authors/roy/transcript.htm
http://www.indymedia.org/print.php3?article_id=231238
http://www.hereinreality.com/carlyle.html

Best international news sites:

http://www.scoop.co.nz/
http://www.narconews.com/index.html
http://www.albawaba.com/news/index.php3?sid=243117&lang=e&dir=news
http://www.timewedo.com/
http://www.colombiareport.org/index.htm
http://www.bluegreenearth.com/
http://www.globalspin.org/world_news_sources.html
http://www.khilafah.com/home/lographics/index.php
http://www.iran-daily.com/daily.shtml
http://english.pravda.ru/

Best news digests:

http://globalcircle.net/00globalization.htm
http://www.informationclearinghouse.info/index.html
http://newsinsider.cjb.net/
http://www.davidcogswell.com/
http://www.lewisnews.com/
http://truthout.com/

Best medical sites:

http://www.whale.to/index.htm
http://redflagsweekly.com/index.html
http://www.mercola.com/index.htm
http://www.tetrahedron.org/
http://www.vaclib.org/
http://www.naturodoc.com/library/public_health/truth_re_smallpox_vaccine.htm

Best education site:

http://www.johmann.net/

Best blog site:

http://xymphora.blogspot.com/

Best chatrooms:

http://www.rumormillnews.net/
http://www.jumeirahbeach.com/

Best all-purpose publication:

http://www.wired.com/wired/current.html

Best mind control sites:

http://www.heart7.net/mcf/index.htm
http://www.trance-formation.com/NewMain.htm

Best humanitarian site:

http://www.nonviolence.org/vitw/

Best Bush sites:

http://www.awolbush.com/
http://www.disinfo.com/pages/dossier/id195/pg1/
http://www.dcia.com/ic.html
http://www.allhatnocattle.net/new_page_1.htm
http://www.campaignwatch.org/more1.htm
http://www.tarpley.net/bush2.htm
http://www.nathanielblumberg.com/neil.htm

Best election sites:

http://www.talion.com/vote-rigging.html
http://www.vote.org/fraud.htm
http://Votescam.com/chap1.html

Best newsletters you can get only in e-mail form:

(sign up for all of them)
GlobalCirclenet mailto:webmaster@globalcircle.net
CCW mailto:ccw@wolfenet.com
MUTANEX Communications mailto:mutanex@aloha.net
Preventive Psychiatry eNewsletter mailto:
gkohls@cpinternet.com

Best online books:

http://gary.webb.home.attbi.com/wsb/html/
view.cgi-home.html-.html
http://www.balkanunity.org/mideast/english/zionism/
http://www.mega.nu:8080/ampp/sutton_wall_street/
http://www.constitution.org/ocbpt/ocbpt.htm
http://www.edge.org/documents/ThirdCulture/d-Contents.html
http://www.viewzone.com/tells-all53.html

Best talk radio shows:

http://www.rense.com/
http://www.Meria.net
http://www.infowars.com/
http://www.rise4news.net/

One of the best stories you can read off the bat is: http://www.questionsquestions.net/gatekeepers.html, because it details how many popular left websites such as Common Dreams, The Nation, The Progressive, Z magazine, Alternet, and Tom Paine are tainted by subterranean connections to the CIA. Almost all of them write little about 9/11 and won't even entertain the notion that the tragedies were generated by forces within the U.S. government, making them suspiciously useless in my mind.

Start reading and learn as much as you can. Our collective future depends on it.

About the Author

John Kaminski is a veteran of thirty years in the newspaper business who now finds himself unemployable by most papers because of both what they have become and what he has become.

With the ascent of corporate chains, independent thought has been eliminated from most newspapers as their priority has changed from reporting the news to selling products by exploiting commercial stereotypes.

After three decades of seeing the same old tired formulas twist real news into the partisan pap of profit-oriented publishers, Kaminski learned the mainstream media were not to be trusted under any circumstances. They had ceased to be the vehicles that journalists aspired to work for, and instead had turned into something evil, a part of someone's greater mind-control conspiracy, where the actual truth about many events is simply not allowed.

It is this sense of profound mistrust and skepticism of the official version of events that Kaminski has tapped into and won a large and appreciative audience with his Internet essays on a variety of websites throughout the world.

This selection of 27 essays is culled from the 54 he has written during the past year and upholds what he hopes are the finest traditions of journalism worldwide: speak truth to power and its terror will one day be unraveled.

Longtime followers of his work will see these commentaries as merely a continuation of his earlier efforts, for which he led a previously unremarkable New Hampshire entertainment weekly to an Utne Reader award nomination. This was followed by his own publication, *The New England Pilgrim,* the first publication anywhere to point out that the U.S. government was intimately involved with the 1993 World Trade Center bombing, and that sanctions against Iraq were—and are—a clear violation of the Geneva Conventions.

Both of these, and so many other things, are items which are virtually unknown to the general public, and it is to these matters and others like them that Kaminski devotes his attention, for the betterment of his fellow lifeforms, rather than the exploitation of them.

If You Liked This Book, You Won't Want To Miss Other Titles By Dandelion Books

Available now and always through www.dandelionbooks.net and affiliated websites!!

Non-Fiction:

America, Awake! We Must Take Back Our Country, by Norman D. Livergood . . . This book is intended as a wake-up call for Americans, as Paul Revere awakened the Lexington patriots to the British attack on April 18, 1775, and as Thomas Paine's *Common Sense* roused apathetic American colonists to recognize and struggle against British oppression. Our current situation is similar to that which American patriots faced in the 1770s: a country ruled by 'foreign' and 'domestic' plutocratic powers and a divided citizenry uncertain of their vital interests. (ISBN 189330227X)

The Awakening of An American: How America Broke My Heart, by Meria Heller, with a Foreword by Catherine Austin Fitts . . . A collection of choice interviews from Meria Heller's world-famous www.meria.net rapidly growing radio network that reaches millions of people daily. Dr. Arun Gandhi, Greg Palast, Vincent Bugliosi, Mark Elsis, William Rivers Pitt, Mark Rechtenwald, Nancy Oden & Bob Fertik, Howard Winant, Linda Starr, Dave Chandler, Bev Conover, John Nichols, Robert McChesney, Norman Solomon, Stan Goff and Mark Crispin Miller. (ISBN 189302393)

America's Nightmare: The Presidency of George Bush II, by John Stanton & Wayne Madsen . . . Media & Language, War & Weapons, Internal Affairs and a variety of other issues pointing out the US "crisis without precedent" that was wrought by the US Presidential election of 2000 followed by 9/11. "Stanton & Madsen will challenge many of the things you've been told by CNN and Fox news. This book is dangerous." (ISBN 1893302296)

Seeds Of Fire: China And The Story Behind The Attack On America, by Gordon Thomas . . . The inside story about China that no one can afford to ignore. Using his unsurpassed contacts in Israel,

Washington, London and Europe, Gordon Thomas, internationally acclaimed best-selling author and investigative reporter for over a quarter-century, reveals information about China's intentions to use the current crisis to launch itself as a super-power and become America's new major enemy . . . *"This has been kept out of the news agenda because it does not suit certain business interests to have that truth emerge . . . Every patriotic American should buy and read this book . . . it is simply revelatory."* — (Ray Flynn, Former U.S. Ambassador to the Vatican). (ISBN 1893302547)

Shaking the Foundations: Coming Of Age In The Postmodern Era, by John H. Brand, D.Min., J.D. . . . Scientific discoveries in the Twentieth Century require the restructuring of our understanding the nature of Nature and of human beings. In simple language the author explains how significant implications of quantum mechanics, astronomy, biology and brain physiology form the foundation for new perspectives to comprehend the meaning of our lives. (ISBN 1893302253)

Rebuilding the Foundations: Forging A New And Just America, by John H. Brand, D.Min., J.D. . . . Should we expect a learned scholar to warn us about our dangerous reptilian brains that are the real cause of today's evils? Although Brand is not without hope for rescuing America, he warns us to act fast–and now. Evil men intent on imposing their political, economic, and religious self-serving goals on America are not far from achieving their goal of mastery." (ISBN 1893302334)

Democracy Under Siege: The Jesuits' Attempt To Destroy the Popular Government Of The United States; The True Story of Abraham Lincoln's Death; Banned For Over 100 Years, This Information Now Revealed For The First Time! by C.T. Wilcox . . . U.S. President Lincoln was the triumphant embodiment of the New Concept of Popular Government. Was John Wilkes Booth a Jesuit patsy, hired to do the dirty work for the Roman Catholic church – whose plan, a well-kept secret until now – was to overthrow the American Government? (ISBN 189302318)

The Last Days Of Israel, by Barry Chamish . . . With the Middle East crisis ongoing, *The Last Days of Israel* takes on even greater significance as an important book of our age. Barry Chamish, investigative reporter who has the true story about Yitzak Rabin's assassination, tells it like it is. (ISBN 1893302164)

Fiction:

Freedom: Letting Go Of Anxiety And Fear Of The Unknown, by Jim Britt . . . Jeremy Carter, a fireman from Missouri who is in New York City for the day, decides to take a tour of the Trade Center, only to watch in shock, the attack on its twin towers from a block away. Afterward as he gazes at the pit of rubble and talks with many of the survivors, Jeremy starts to explore the inner depths of his soul, to ask questions he'd never asked before. This dialogue helps him learn who he is and what it takes to overcome the fear, anger, grief and anxiety this kind of tragedy brings. (ISBN1893302741)

The Prince Must Die, by Gower Leconfield . . . breaks all taboos for mystery thrillers. After the "powers that be" suppressed the manuscripts of three major British writers, Dandelion Books breaks through with a thriller involving a plot to assassinate Prince Charles. *The Prince Must Die* brings to life a Britain of today that is on the edge with race riots, neo-Nazis, hard right backlash and neo-punk nihilists. Riveting entertainment . . . you won't be able to put it down. (ISBN 1893302725)

Daniela, by Stephen Weeks . . . A gripping epic novel of sexual obsession and betrayal as Nazi Prague falls. The harboring of deadly secrets and triumph of an enduring love against the hardest of times. Nikolei is a Polish/Ukrainian Jew who finds himself fighting among the Germans then turning against them to save Prague in 1945. Nikolei manages to hide himself among the Germans with a woman working as a prostitute. (ISBN 1893302377)

Unfinished Business, by Elizabeth Lucas Taylor . . . Lindsay Mayer knows something is amiss when her husband, Griffin, a college professor, starts spending too much time at his office and out-of-town. Shortly after the ugly truth surfaces, Griffin disappears altogether. Lindsay is shattered. Life without Griffin is life without life . . . One of the sexiest books you'll ever read! (ISBN 1893302687)

The Woman With Qualities, by Sarah Daniels . . . South Florida isn't exactly the Promised Land that forty-nine-year-old newly widowed Keri Anders had in mind when she transplanted herself here from the northeast . . . A tough action-packed novel that is far more than a love story. (ISBN 1893302113)

Weapon In Heaven, by David Bulley . . . Eddy Licklighter is in a fight with God for his very own soul. You can't mess around half-assed when fighting with God. You've got to go at it whole-hearted. Eddy loses his wife and baby girl in a fire. Bulley's protagonist is a contemporary version of the Old Testament character of Job. Licklighter wants nothing from God except His presence so he can kill him off. The humor, warmth, pathos and ultimate redemption of Licklighter will make you hold your sides with laughter at the same time you shed common tears for his "God-awful" dilemma. (ISBN1893302288)

Adventure Capital, by John Rushing . . . South Florida adventure, crime and violence in a fiction story based on a true life experience. A book you will not want to put down until you reach the last page. (ISBN 1893302083)

A Mother's Journey: To Release Sorrow And Reap Joy, by Sharon Kay . . . A poignant account of Norah Ann Mason's life journey as a wife, mother and single parent. This book will have a powerful impact on anyone, female or male, who has experienced parental abuse, family separations, financial struggles and a desperate need to find the magic in life that others talk about that just doesn't seem to be there for them. (ISBN 1893302520)

ALL DANDELION BOOKS ARE AVAILABLE THROUGH WWW.DANDELIONBOOKS.NET AND AFFILIATED WEBSITES . . . ALWAYS.